More Praise for
Essentials of Balanced Scorecard

"For everyone out there who hasn't ⅴ⁻⁺ ⁻ ⁻ ⁻ed score card phenomenon exists and tion, here is your cheat sheet. Nair ⅼ and writes in a way that is both com

—Patrick Lenc
Author, The Five Dysfunctions of a Team
President, The Table Group

"Mohan Nair paints a unique picture for Balanced Scorecard. He moves beyond the what and how to describe an operating philosphy for implementation. If you need to improve your organization, take the first step and read this book."

—Steve Sharp
Chairman
Triquint Semiconductor

"Mr. Nair's exploration of Balanced Scorecard is particularly effective and useful because he remains grounded with the practical reality of running a business and the importance of cohesive but simple measures in driving successful execution of core strategies."

—Mark Ganz
President
Regence Group

"A practical and foundation book for the people in your organization who don't spend their days on BSC but must be convinced. It provides reach to others who have not experienced BSC in an understandable language from an author who has been running companies."

—Professor Bala Balachandran
Distinguished Professor of Accounting and
Information Systems and Decision Sciences
Kellogg School of Management

ESSENTIALS
of Balanced Scorecard

Essentials Series

The Essentials Series was created for busy business advisory and corporate professionals. The books in this series were designed so that these busy professionals can quickly acquire knowledge and skills in core business areas.

Each book provides need-to-have fundamentals for those professionals who must:

- Get up to speed quickly, because they have been promoted to a new position or have broadened their responsibility scope
- Manage a new functional area
- Brush up on new developments in their area of responsibility
- Add more value to their company or clients

Other books in this series include:

For more information on any of the above titles, please visit *www.wiley.com*

ESSENTIALS

of Balanced Scorecard

Mohan Nair

John Wiley & Sons, Inc.

For general information on our other products and services, or technical support, please contact our Customer Care Department within the United States at 800-762-2974, outside the United States at 317-572-3993 or fax 317-572-4002.

Note: Portions of this book are adapted from *Activity-Based Information Systems: An Executive's Guide to Implementation* by Mohan Nair (New York: John Wiley & Sons, Inc., 1999).

Wiley also publishes its books in a variety of electronic formats. Some content that appears in print may not be available in electronic books.

For more information about Wiley products, visit our Web site at *www.wiley.com*.

Library of Congress Cataloging-in-Publication Data:

Nair, Mohan.
    Essentials of balanced scorecard / Mohan Nair.
       p. cm. — (Essentials series)
  Includes bibliographical references and index.
    ISBN 0-471-56973-9 (pbk.)
      1. Industrial productivity—Measurement. 2. Strategic planning.
  3. Organizational effectiveness—Evaluation. I. Title. II. Series.
  HD56.25 .N35 2004
  658.4'012—dc22

                2003027402

Printed in the United States of America

10 9 8 7 6 5 4 3 2 1

About the Author

Mohan Nair is CEO of Emerge Inc., an advisory firm focused on strategy and corporate performance management. Identified as an adventure capitalist, Nair has founded two companies, a venture capital firm, and has taken high-profile executive roles in four high-technology companies. Most recently, Nair served as director, president, and Chief Operating Officer of ABC Technologies. He serves on several non-profit boards including the AeA. For seven years, he taught as an adjunct professor at J.L. Kellogg School of Management at Northwestern University of Chicago, and his articles have appeared in numerous publications including *Byte Magazine*, *The Journal of Corporate Accounting and Finance*, and *The Journal of Cost and Performance Management*. A highly requested speaker, Nair has been profiled or quoted in *Forbes, Industry Week, Business Finance*, and *CNBC-Asia*. He is author of *Activity-Based Information Systems: An Executive's Guide to Implementation* (Wiley).

I thank my wife, Charu, for believing in this book project. Your support is immensely appreciated.
I thank my mother for her love and belief in me. Your contribution to the world is immeasurable.
I ask my loving dog to forgive me because she sacrificed many walks over a year.
I thank my daughter, Anushka, who saw her daddy work on the laptop for many nights.
I dedicate this book to you.

Contents

Contents

Preface

Balanced Scorecard (BSC) is not about strategy; it is about making strategy actionable. As the title declares, "Essentials of Balanced Scorecard" is designed to assist you in understanding the fundamentals of Balanced Scorecard.

It takes a great deal of complex actions to present ideas simply. Simplicity is the guiding principle behind this book. After some years of presenting ideas and learning, I have found that today's executives have very little time to dig through metaphors and fancy symbolisms to get their facts. They prefer the truth in two-plus pages with diagrams. Unfortunately, justice cannot serve this topic with just two pages and diagrams. But I have tried to make the book simple to approach and use. Hopefully, you will be able to pick up this book and find it easy to read and digest (approach), as well as simple to return as reference (use).

About This Book

Essentials of Balanced Scorecard is designed for the executive-level reader who is relatively impatient with the verbosity. Balanced Scorecard has moved at an astounding adoption rate. Other analytic applications like activity-based cost/management (ABC/M), budgeting, and planning, customer relationship management (CRM), and supply-chain management (SCM) took the normal paths of recognition and adoption and took years before they had enterprisewide use. Credit goes to its founders Professor Robert Kaplan and David Norton, who designed the system with execution in mind. The demand for this methodology seems to have filled the inherently unfilled needs for the CEOs and the corporations they serve:

- The need for making strategy actionable at all levels
- The need to balance objectives and measures and to isolate cause-and-effect relationships in the work being done to attain a strategic purpose
- The need to relate vision, mission, and values to strategy
- The need to move beyond just financial measures to their underlying measures

There was also another need that was hiding under the wings: The need to bring a framework to strategy and execution as well as the need to bring together all the disparate analytic and measurement systems in a corporation under one framework or conceptual umbrella.

How This Book Is Organized

Essentials of Balanced Scorecard is organized in modular chapters. It is suggested that you read the chapters in sequence for consistency in conceptual models that are being developed. But if you have a basic familiarity with the topic, you can use the book as a reference document by diving into specific chapters you feel are relevant. In discussing the content and focus of each chapter, the unique approach of the book will surface:

Chapter 1: Overview. What is the difference between monitoring, measuring, managing, and direction setting? Know what the blind spots in business are? Understand the strategic paradox set up in business and how BSC assists as a solution.

Chapter 2: What Is Balanced Scorecard? What is Balanced Scorecard? Why the methodology balances and influences? What is a strategic thrust? What is performance measurement?

What are the four perspectives behind the balanced scorecard methodology? What is strategy mapping and its relationship to cause and effect?

Chapter 3: From Management to Performance Management. Why is information no longer power? What are data obesity and knowledge starvation? What is the nature of information and its behavior? What brings relevance to information—the ecosystem that feeds a Balanced Scorecard? What are performance measures? And what are their types? What are the differences between leading and lagging indicators? What is the relationship between co-related and non-co-related indicators? What are the main perspectives in BSC—namely financial, customer, internal, and learning and growth? What are targets, measures, initiatives, and objectives?

Chapter 4: Mission, Vision, Values: The Precursor to Balanced Scorecard. What are the many definitions of strategy? Why is strategy important to BSC? What are the key elements of strategy? Why strategy is not operational excellence? What is a mission? What is vision? What are values? Why are mission, vision, and values important to BSC?

Chapter 5: Six Success Factors to Implementing Balanced Scorecard. This is an overview of the six factors and how they work together to enable a successful BSC endeavor.

Chapter 6: Success Factor One: Understand Self. Understand how to identify your organizational readiness for change. Know how to identify if your change-leader's personality fits the task at hand. Is the CEO and management team ready to institutionalize BSC? What is task-relevant leadership? What is task-relevant readiness?

Chapter 7: Success Factor Two: Understand the Balanced Scorecard Learning Cycle. Do you know what the four stages of development of BSC in the organization are? Understand the characteristics of the education, pilot, and enterprise phase of development? Know how technology enables the five phases of BSC growth in the organization? Differentiate between a fad and long-term transformation.

Chapter 8: Success Factor Three: Know the Road Map for Implementation. What are the characteristics of a doomed BSC exercise? How do you implement a BSC project? What is the road map for activities around a BSC system?

Chapter 9: Success Factor Four: Treat Balanced Scorecard as a Project. Know how to treat a BSC exercise as a project using project management fundamentals and product introduction skills. Understand why the needs of users increase. Define a project schedule with deliverables. Identify overall project guidelines and system design. Discover how to develop a set of deliverables in a phased approach to the BSC project. Learn to define the level of involvement for each consultant and vendor. Uncover how to build and manage a performance measures dictionary. Learn to establish a tools inventory.

Chapter 10: Success Factor Five: Use Technology as an Enabler. Know the three classes of BSC systems. Learn the common subsystems of any BSC system and find out how to decide on which software vendor to work with.

Chapter 11: Success Factor Six: Cascade the Scorecard. Why cascade the scorecard? What are the benefits of enterprisewide BSC? What are the challenges to developing an enterprisewide BSC implementation?

Chapter 12: Eleven Deadly Sins of Balanced Scorecard. The eleven deadly sins of scorecarding need to be understood and conquered:

- Five people-related sins
- Three process-related sins
- Three technology-related sins

Chapter 13: The Ultimate Partnership: Balanced Scorecard and Performance Management. Performance management is the larger umbrella for BSC and all other analytic applications. Find out how BSC assists in framing performance management. Uncover where BSC can assist organizations with unique new application demands.

Glossary. Common terms used in the book that may need further definition.

Suggested Readings. Suggested articles and books for further reference and learning.

How to Use This Book

The book is focused on practical tips and examples. Be sure to check out the boxed sections within each chapter:

- *Tips and Techniques.* Keys to unlocking the practical accelerators in implementing Balanced Scorecard.
- *In the Real World.* Examples of real organizations and their efforts in performance management and Balanced Scorecard.

This book is focused on implementing Balanced Scorecard with an eye to people, process, and technology.

Acknowledgments

I write my second book in the field of corporate performance management because the topic has significant impact to businesses worldwide. The temptations to describe strategy formulation and realization were too great to ignore. But the writing of a book takes sacrifice from others more than me. I have many people to acknowledge but here are a few that I must mention:

- Pat Cox, CEO, Francisco Garybayo, and Vicky Bailey, from Qsent, for their kind support throughout the creation and development of the book. I thank the Qsent team for always reminding me that my book was of value to them.

- Thanks for the personal interviews:
  - Steve Sharp, Chairman of Triquint Semiconductor, for his confidence in me.
  - John Harker, CEO of InFocus Systems, for his constant support.
  - Treasure Bailey, Director HR InFocus Systems, for granting me a personal interview.
  - Dr. Deborah Kerr, chief strategy officer for the state of Texas' auditor's office, for her belief that my work contributes to the industry.
  - Mark Ganz, CEO of the Regence Group, for his personal encouragement, belief, and trust in my work.

- Candace Petersen, VP Marketing, InFocus Systems, for her guidance.

- Brent Bullock, Partner at Perkins Coie LLC, for his advice and help whenever I needed it.
- Special thanks to Wayne Embree and Ted Bernhard, partners at Cascadia Partners, for their constant belief in me and for always being friends first.
- Special thanks to Mike Tipping, CEO of Panorama Business Views, for the use and reference to case studies. Also thanks to Lynn Myers, Joy Kalajainen, and Jennifer Eisa for all the follow-up and responses to my questions.
- Thanks to Gary Weeks, Jeff Tryens, and Governor Ted Kulongowski, for allowing me to share in the Oregon Performance and Accountability initiative.

This book is the result of many years of learning and study but would not happen if it were not for the work of Sheck Cho, my Editor along with the Wiley & Sons team. I thank you for your dedication to your craft.

MOHAN NAIR

Emerge® Inc.
P.O. Box 1222
Lake Oswego, Oregon 97035
www.2emerge.com
mohan@2emerge.com

ESSENTIALS
of Balanced Scorecard

CHAPTER 1

Overview

After reading this chapter, you will be able to

- Understand what the difference is between monitoring, measuring, managing, and direction setting.
- Understand why the essence of Balanced Scorecard is not measurement but direction setting.
- Know what the blind spots in business are.
- Understand the strategic paradox set up in business and how BSC assists as a solution.

Ancient cultures recognized the importance of measuring the passage of time, as well as the need for standards for recording transactions and communication. They were preoccupied with measuring time, size, and weight. Records show that the Babylonians and the Egyptians measured days and months more than 5,000 years ago. Many used the celestial bodies as a guide to these measurements.

The challenges of travel to far-off lands over the water brought about the greatest of all obstacles. Many a ship sank because its crew lacked the understanding of where they were with respect to land. By 150 A.D., however, Ptolemy had reduced the known world into 27 maps,[1] and created the first world atlas, which greatly aided ships in navigation. He knew of latitude easily because the equator was right in the middle of the earth. Zero degrees longitude was the true challenge.

Longitude had to be measured using time—that is, both time at land and current time. It took John Harrison, working between 1730 and

1770, to look beyond the stars (the tools of Galileo and Isaac Newton) and find the mechanical timepieces that could withstand the hazards of travel.

Essence of Balanced Scorecard

Just as great ships must chart their position before undergoing ocean voyages, businesses must measure their position before knowing their direction. The challenge has been in finding the tools to measure these organization's "voyage." The true fallacy of measurement is that it is not an end but a means to a new beginning. Measurement is the driver of the next direction, not just the documenter of today's position.

But measurement has gotten a bad rap. It is viewed as punishment in management clothing. If you call it *accountability*, many believe it to be accounting and a precursor for layoffs. The operational value of measurement has been accepted in manufacturing but when accountants walk the floor, measurement takes an entirely new branding.

Business needs measurement that can sustain the changing tides of the climate of commerce. Businesses hunger for a framework to measure its location in the continuous journey to its final destination or goal. From this measurement comes the rudder of management, and from the rudder comes direction.

Balanced Scorecard (BSC) is born from this rich history of measurement and serves the same purpose to business as the timepiece served the ancient mariners. BSC attempts to move businesses from monitoring to measurement; from measurement to management and from management to direction setting:

- *Monitoring.* The art and science of observing employee behavior and coaching
- *Measurement.* The art and science of gauging, using numbers and metrics, performance to a task

- *Management.* The art and science of motivating, coaching, and enabling individuals and teams in the achievement of an objective
- *Direction setting.* The art and science of discovering strategic directions that are unique and differentiating in the marketplace, communicating this to all levels in the organization in the form that they can identify and co-relate their day-to-day actions to the goals

Many organizations are fearful of measurement because it symbolizes accountability and, in some ways, documents a weapon to terminate employees.

But if we believed ourselves to be in the same boat, trying to take on a new journey to a new land, we would measure where we are and how far we have to go. The basis for any action plan is knowledge. Knowledge, using Balanced Scorecard, is purposeful and focused on strategic action—that is, translating strategy into day-to-day action plans and initiatives.

Why Balanced Scorecard?

Corporations, both big and small, can fail for several reasons. But the most significant cause of failure is not a lack of strategy, but the incapacity to execute on a balanced strategy. Balanced Scorecard exists to serve this incapacity.

Its founders, Professor Robert Kaplan, from Harvard Business School, and David Norton, a consultant, put together a research study to evaluate and understand new methods for measuring performance. They assembled key organizations to help them formulate this understanding. The teams set about to formulate a new method that would not rely so much on just financial metrics as measure but would show a balance of financial and nonfinancial perspectives. The outcome of this process is

TIPS & TECHNIQUES

Now more than 50 percent of the Fortune 1000 and 40 percent of companies in Europe use a form of the BSC according to Bain & Co.[a] In addition to this, Balanced Scorecard serves to bridge several other dichotomous elements of strategy. Organizations are asking fundamental questions about their strategy and have come to realize that balance in strategic objectives is key to making strategy actionable. Without this balance, most of the organization seems not represented in strategy. Consider the following key questions to understand if BSC is for your organization:

- Is our strategy one-sided and only focused on financial gains and targets?
- How do we know if the measures that we review are looking farther ahead or just lagging indicators of past performance?
- Do our measures and goals cover all aspects of the enterprise, or are they just based on the structure of our corporation, that is, are they just data from silos of business units measuring their unique targets?
- Do we really understand what drives our business?
- Do we have a handle on what actions cause other results?

[a] Andra Gumbus and Bridget Lyons, "The Balanced Scorecard at Phillips Electronics," *Strategic Finance*, access at *www.bettermanagement.com/library*.

the Balanced Scorecard.[2] It is *formalism*, a method that translates strategic themes to actionable and measurable objectives that are ready for execution at all levels of the organization.

In good times, profits soar and corporations seldom care why or what causes success. Often, they believe that being in the "right place, right time" is O.K. When these businesses turn sour, they scramble for answers. It seems that, in great times, corporations don't listen to anything. When times get rough, they seem to listen to everyone and use any method to get themselves out of trouble.

Management is the art of knowing how and what to deploy during both rough and good times because management is acyclic in behavior. Balanced Scorecard is one such methodology that identifies and formalizes the main drivers to the business and provides a quick view of your corporation's strategic health.

Balanced Scorecard is focused on uncovering the main nonfinancial drivers of the business, along with the economics of the business. Balanced Scorecard shows you a way to make strategy actionable. As a framework for action, it can be updated and creates a renewable methodology and framework.

Consider Exhibit 1.1, which illustrates the issues surrounding a strategic framework for action. Usually, strategic planning exercises drive for aligning *vision, mission, values,* and *strategy.* They also discuss items such as competencies, strengths, weaknesses and opportunities, and threats. This method is often called SWOT analysis, which is a way for organizations

EXHIBIT 1.1

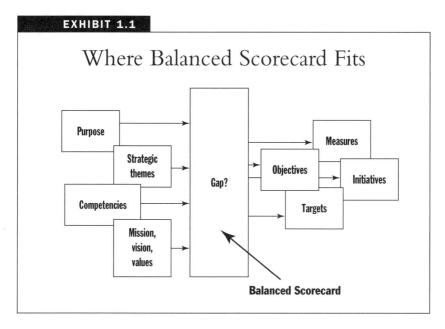

Where Balanced Scorecard Fits

to ensure that all elements of the business are incorporated into a strategic plan in the marketplace. Hence, the exercise usually covers the internal and external challenges that a corporation is facing and will face, in an attempt to look ahead and find the next big thing.

Meanwhile, the corporation is running along driving to current measures at the operational level, and the challenge comes when the senior management wishes to drive new strategies into the organization. BSC fits this purpose of providing a framework for aligning strategy to the tactics, with corresponding objectives and measures. Exhibit 1.1 shows the gap filled by the BSC.

Business of Blindspots

Corporations have always measured things that matter to them. Hence, to claim that any methodology enables the measurement of the *right* things is ludicrous and somewhat condescending to preceding methods that have been introduced.

It would seem that corporations sometimes measure too much of some things and too little of others. It would also seem that many of these measurements are unintegrated, serve the wrong goals, and form a paradox within the corporation where forms of measurement compete with each other, falling short of the overall strategic goals of the corporation. Many corporations lack an overarching model for monitoring, measuring and managing the business. Balanced Scorecard offers a broad and overarching skin to the structural architecture of the business.

Avoiding Strategic Paradox

There are two forms of *strategic paradox* in strategy formulation and execution:

1. Mistakenly viewing strategy as operational effectiveness
2. Mistakenly assuming that strategy and actions in an organization are always aligned

According to Professor Michael Porter, strategy has been viewed in the context of *operational effectiveness*. Using the language of activities, he has outlined a way to differentiate between strategic positioning and operational effectiveness.[3] Using activities, operational effectiveness is performing similar activities better than rivals, while strategic positioning is performing different activities or performing similar activities differently. When organizations do anything that appears to be a competitive advantage using operational effectiveness, others often follow. W. Chan Kim, Boston Consulting Group Bruce D. Henderson professor of International Management at INSEAD in Fontainbleau, France, and Renee Mauborgne, a senior research fellow at INSEAD, put it well: "The trouble with forging a highway is that if you are right, imitators will follow. Then you are back into protecting your base and become subject to conventional wisdom."[4] Professor Porter emphasizes that benchmarking only makes companies similar. Porter emphasizes the value of strategic positioning over operational effectiveness (see Chapter 4). Just using Balanced Scorecard to identify and improve the activities in a company of the business does not forge a competitive advantage. However, there is tremendous value in using BSC to align the entire organization to strategy.

Finding Competency in Strategy Alignment

Many executives lock themselves in conference rooms or resort hotel rooms to uncover their organizational strategy. But strategy formulated with no regard to strengths and weaknesses in capability is blind strategy. The true power of strategy can only be expressed in work performed. Hence, the real challenge seems to be, not only strategy formulation, but also the ability to create an operational framework to execute the strategy. Many executives tell me that the most important competency of all is the competency of being able to execute on goals.

Furthermore, the business world is guided by *change*. And change can affect business models drastically. Mergers and acquisitions can transform the competitive landscape as power shifts. Hence, sticking to a good-looking strategy when strategic variables change can be dangerous. For companies to be effective, they must have as much ability to change their strategy as to formulate one. This is characterized by several capabilities:

- The ability to formulate strategic thrusts or themes—that is, several key strategic differentiable objectives for focus and strength
- The ability to institutionalize and operationalize these thrusts into key activities or sets of activities if performed would enhance and enable the key strategy
- The ability to change the emphasis and manage resources of these strategic thrusts adapting the underlying set of activities quickly

Strategy without strategic alignment to key organizational activities renders organizations impotent. The strength of a resilient organization comes from its ability to change its strategic thrust and reflect it in actions and corresponding performance measures. This connection between strategy, strategic thrusts, and activities can be achieved using BSC. For example, consider a high-technology CRM company that competes in the fast-paced contact information business. This company might have the following elements to strategy alignment:

- *Strategy.* Dominate, with 60 percent share, the XYZ market by building a direct consumer focus.
- *Strategic thrusts*
  - Be the leader in direct consumer marketing.
  - Establish and dominate in customer service.
  - Align with larger player by providing the most reliable CRM subsystems for them.
- *Key activities.* Activities serving strategic thrust are
  - (a1, a2, a4)
  - (a4, a5, a8)
  - (a4, a9, a7) where a = key activity like "provide contact management at lowest cost"

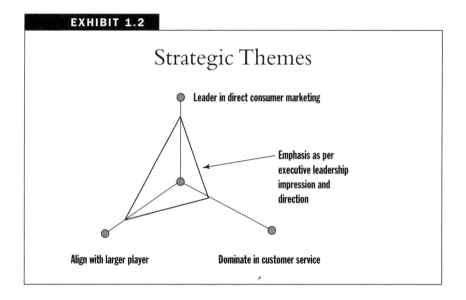

EXHIBIT 1.2

Strategic Themes

Exhibit 1.2 illustrates such a strategy with emphasis in order of priority.

Michael Tracy and Fred Wiersema,[5] authors of *Discipline of Market Leaders*, list three strategic thrusts to market leaders:

1. Operational excellence

2. Product leadership

3. Customer intimacy

Various sets of activities, if optimized and combined in the right way, can make these themes actionable. Meanwhile, management will establish the priority of the strategic thrusts as shown in the Exhibit 1.2.

In actual truth, the emphasis of activities with respect to the themes is shown by the dashed lines in Exhibit 1.3. This exhibit illustrates the organization's focus with respect to its emphasis on one axis or the other. For example, the organization states that its focus is customer over operational power. A Paradox Map compares where resources should be emphasized to achieve the strategy of the company against what work is currently being performed.

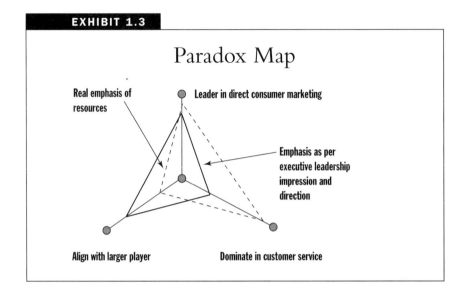

EXHIBIT 1.3

Paradox Map

Real emphasis of resources

Leader in direct consumer marketing

Emphasis as per executive leadership impression and direction

Align with larger player

Dominate in customer service

One of the greatest challenges that BSC solves is misalignment between the strategy and the real work being performed. BSC avoids the strategic paradox in which the CEO thinks the strategy is working in action when in actuality, the strategy and the real work, as defined by the activities of the organization, are not working in concert.

As Craig Weatherup of PepsiCo claimed, eventually strategy leads to processes because "capability comes only by combining a competence with a reliable process."[6] Strategy is realized in the unique combination of activities and processes, but the key tool for aligning strategy and the primary activities of an organization is the Balanced Scorecard.

Summary

Balanced Scorecard serves the needs of a large portion of the Fortune 1000 who are in deep need of making strategy actionable. BSC is also designed to ensure that performance metrics and strategic themes are balanced with financial and nonfinancial, operational and financial, leading and lagging indicators.

Organizations seek to translate strategy to key actions. A syndrome among many companies called strategic paradox can slow progress. This syndrome manifests itself in the form of disparate, disconnected actions in the core of a company when the upper management believes that the company is acting on a strategy and that the strategy and actions in the organization are always aligned. The paradox expresses itself as a misunderstood strategy. Balanced Scorecard attempts to remove this paradox and align all activities to the true purpose of the strategy.

CHAPTER 2

What Is Balanced Scorecard?

After reading this chapter, you will be able to

- Understand what a Balanced Scorecard is.
- Understand why the methodology balances the factors that influence strategy.
- Understand what a strategic thrust or theme is.
- Understand what corporate performance measurement is.
- Understand the four perspectives behind the Balance Scorecard methodology.
- Understand what strategy mapping is and its relationship to cause and effect.

As the name implies, Balanced Scorecard (BSC) is a methodology to solve challenges in balancing the theories of a strategy with its execution. It has the following characteristics:

- Its methodology is suited for managing business strategy.
- It uses a common language at all levels of the organization.
- Is uses a common set of principles to manage day-to-day operations as well as to framework the company's strategy.
- It is designed to identify and manage business purposes.

- It provides a balance between certain relatively opposing forces in strategy:
  - Internal and external influences
  - Leading and lagging indicators and measures
  - Financial and nonfinancial goals
  - Organizational silos focused on their own goals and an overarching framework of goals
  - Finance priorities and operations
- It aligns strategic goals with objectives, targets, and metrics.
- It cascades to all levels of the organization.

In a nutshell, then, BSC takes strategy from theory to action. BSC is not a measurement system per se; it is a directional tool for translating strategy into action at all levels of the organization. At its root is the principle of *motivated action*—that is, granting the individuals and teams within the organization the ability to know that their actions feed a strategic focus every day. Measurement, often the first thing that comes to mind when considering scorecards, is really second to this principle. Great corporations believe in measurement, but only as a motivating instrument.

Just as important, BSC has been shown to be effective as a foundation to good management practices beyond measurement and scoring. A Chartered Institute of Personnel and Development (CIPD) three-year study was targeted at understanding how good management practices influence performance. Twelve companies were observed in this study—companies whose employees are stimulated to do their jobs and serve customers. Greater performance levels were found in six of the companies. All six used BSC or a comparable method.[1]

An Argument for Balance yet Focus

It is often stated in business that focus is the key to achieving a goal. Hence, the natural effort of senior management is to cut anything that does not fit the goal. Analogies like "being laser-like" or "putting the wood behind the arrow" speak to the ideas of singularity in goals and focus. Some of these analogies actually speak to the art of war and to battle strategies as comparatives. And in fact, on the ground level sales and marketing battles do need this kind of focus. But strategic focus is built on another set of analogies that are more applicable—not a single focus but a focus on specific competencies applied to a small set of strategic themes. On an organizational level, the battle of strategy cannot be one of singular focus, because the elements necessary to perform a strategy demand balance—a balance of activities within the organization to achieve the tactical wins.

British forces in Singapore during World War II focused all their defenses toward the sea to guard against Japanese attacks. Believing that the Japanese would attack from the South China Sea, the British forces were imbalanced in their strategic intent. The Japanese forces, after careful consideration, walked into Singapore via a short three-quarter mile causeway located to the north that connected the Malayan peninsula to Singapore. The Japanese conquered the small but strategic port. The lack of a balanced view of the corporate theater could cause similar results.

Battle strategies teach us that strategic and tactical wins must build momentum and also competencies for future battles. Today, battles are not won the way they were many years ago. Today, forces must win multiple battles at the same time in multiple theaters with limited budget and resources.

Balance between Internal and External Factors

Organizations that build competencies for tomorrow while winning the battles of today are responding to the need for *balance*. Organizations who understand balance acknowledge and exploit both the internal and the external factors when assessing their strategy. Many times, organizations only focus on the internal aspects of their business—that is, the operational aspects of getting product to market but not the challenges of selling and marketing or the condition of the market. Many times, this syndrome is called "build it and they will come."

Balance in Leading and Lagging Indicators

Peter Drucker, founder of modern management, states that "we need measurements for a company or industry that are akin to the 'leading indicators' and 'lagging indicators' that economists have developed during the past half-century to predict the direction in which the economy is likely to move and for how long."[2]

Financial measures found in balance sheets and income statements and other statutory reports are mainly lagging indicators to a business. In other words, they tell you what *has* occurred, not what could. Most data in the news and in the magazines are lagging indicators. Most of the information on past sales, production performance, and so on are lagging indicators of performance because they tell you where you have been and how you have performed. Leading indicators are signs of future performance or situations. For example, if you noticed that your daughter had a fever, using a thermometer that would be a lagging indicator of illness. But if you witnessed your daughter sneezing earlier, or returning home and appearing rather sluggish, that would be a leading indicator. The power of a balanced strategic performance system is to acknowledge both leading and lagging indicators, which allows corporations to balance past results with future drivers of performance.

Balance between Financial and Nonfinancial Measures

Many corporate leaders tend to think in terms of numbers. "Perhaps the most recognizable defect of financial-only goals is the barrier that inevitably blocks the translation of overall corporate financial goals into subgoals that people in the enterprise can pursue with confidence."[3]

They measure progress in financial terms and believe that all financial performance motivates everyone in their organization equally. This cannot be further from the truth. Just as Maslow's hierarchy of needs identifies human performance to be a complex mix of basic and advanced desires and expectations, so is the corporate hierarchy. When organizations frame their strategic themes—that is, what they are going to do with a strategy and how they are to execute it—they must acknowledge the mix between financial and nonfinancial objectives. Balance comes in the form of the careful, calculated sharing of financial and nonfinancial goals weaved into a strategy. We already know that people are not motivated solely by money but the achievement of nonfinancial goals as well, which usually leads to money.

A common misconception is that nonfinancial goals are nonnumeric in nature. That is also not true. Nonfinancial goals can be measured. Even perception can be measured, of course, with a level of inaccuracy. For example, an engineering team discussing the Balanced Scorecard approach was very uncomfortable with the nonfinancial part of the equation because the team believed that the important issues were measurable; the "foo-foo" (emotional) aspects of the program could not be measured and were thus irrelevant. The team leader, after acknowledging the perception, decided that a survey would be generated on how people felt about certain engineering results and that a perception index would be generated as a measure of improvement. The engineering team agreed wholeheartedly with the methodology.

Balance between Organizational Silos and the Overall Corporation

Organizations are challenged with what is the best business architecture for achieving their financial goals. Some believe that independent business units are best while others believe that corporate structures with centralized control are best. Some believe that certain key sustaining functions like human resources and IT should be centralized to enable economies of scale and optimize resources, while others believe that each should be accountable for resources that they can control. These battles have been going on for centuries, and supporters of the various approaches can all find evidence for any one of these architectures working.

For example, the U.S. Marine Corps has long been structured based on the basic business principles rather than business practices. They want independent thinkers in the front line who will be able to be resourceful, while they want strategic leadership from the top. Business principles should drive architecture rather than the other way around. Balanced Scorecard can serve as a strong business principle. Balanced Scorecard assists in the execution of a strategy and can be applied to any organizational structure to provide overriding clarity to strategic intent.

Balance of Finance with Operational Priorities

As long as business has existed, finance has been characterized as "bean-counting" while operations has been associated with actually creating a product or delivering a service. Over the centuries, financial methods have changed to accommodate the evolution in business practice, but one challenge still hinders business—the financial numbers do not reflect what truly goes on in business, and hence, strategy is difficult to measure and manage.

Changes in the character of business assets have exaggerated the challenge even further. In the past, company assets would be reflected on the balance sheet, but now 85 percent of the assets are intangible. Hence, the traditional financial statements only measure the tangible, when the intangible is what fuels the future. A company could produce financial results through a core competency of garnering partnerships, but this capability would not be reflected in the financial reports to shareholders. Of course, the obligatory annual report would declare this advantage in

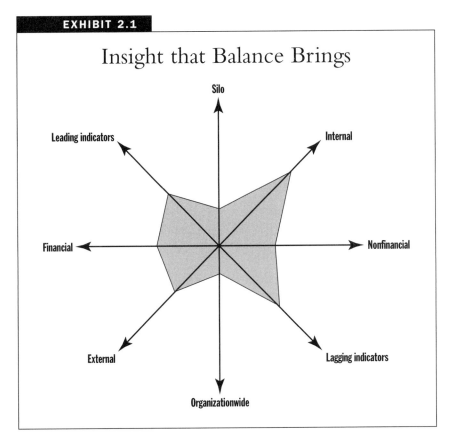

EXHIBIT 2.1

Insight that Balance Brings

several well-photographed pictures of hands-shaking in agreements. But this will not show competency.

Organizations that balance these competencies of financial value measures with operational units are the ones that have placed analytical eyesight to their operational body. Exhibit 2.1 illustrates the balance among all the key performance measures and indicators that underlie the need for BSC. BSC gives corporations this insight.

Four Perspectives of Balanced Scorecard

Professor Robert Kaplan and David Norton declare that strategy is a set of hypotheses about cause and effect in their first book, *Balanced*

Scorecard.[4] Making strategy work in organizations demands that we take advantage of all the competencies within the organization and articulate strategy with several perspectives in mind to ensure that balance is maintained. Kaplan and Norton articulated four perspectives that can guide companies as they translate strategy into actionable terms. They do not argue that these perspectives are necessary and sufficient conditions for success, however. In fact, they recommend these perspectives but suggest that organizations add any perspectives that are more relevant.

1. *Financial perspective*

- What are the financial targets?
- What drives these targets?
- What kind of profit and revenue to achieve?
- In a nonprofit organization, what budget guides you?

2. *Customer perspective*

- Who are the customers?
- How do you delight them?
- What segments do you wish to address?
- What goals do you wish to achieve with partners?
- What are your goals for the distribution channel?

3. *Internal perspective*

- In which processes must we be the best to win customers?
- What internal activities do we need to sustain competencies?

4. *Learning and growth perspective*

- What must we be great in performing, and how do we train our people to get up to that level?
- What climate and culture nurtures growth?
- What do we have to do in developing and training our people to achieve the other objectives?

These perspectives (see Exhibit 2.2) framed with an organization's mission, vision, values, and strategic themes form the Balanced Scorecard ar-

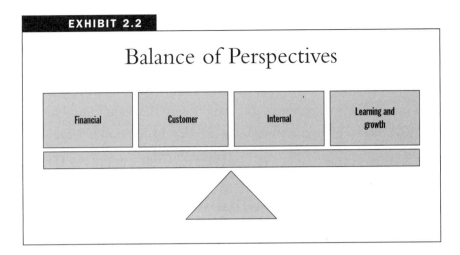

EXHIBIT 2.2

Balance of Perspectives

| Financial | Customer | Internal | Learning and growth |

senal. Before discussing mission, vision, values and strategic themes in Chapter 4, let us consider defining these perspectives.

Financial Perspective

What financial goals need to be achieved to realize your strategic themes and objectives? In a profit-pursuing business, this financial perspective is the more overused and overanalyzed. The revenues, both recurring and new, subscription-based or otherwise, margins, and expenses are very important to an organization seeking to achieve its goals. Frankly, a common mistake with organizations is that they forget the link between the financial goals and the nonfinancial strategy of the company. The financial perspective gives respect to the relationship between stated financial goals and other goals that feed the machine to create the result.

It is important to note that in mission-driven organizations like the U.S. Marine Corps or a nonprofit organization, the mission, not the financial goal, is the overriding target into which all other objectives feed. Or in other cases, "In education, health, and not-for-profit organizations, service, not profit, is the defining characteristic."[5] A good example of this is found with the State of Texas Auditors Office (SAO). Deborah Kerr, SAO chief strategy officer, isolated this challenge of reprioritizing the perspectives and adapted it to reflect the mission as the key driver rather than the financial perspective[6] (for more, see "In the Real World" in Chapters 8 and 10).

Given the profit-pursuing organizations, the financial perspective is critical as it forces recognition and definition to the main critical financial goals that the organization must achieve. In these tough times of business, money might seem like everything, but the financial perspective gives us the following reminders:

- The main goal of business is wealth creation, as measured by a series of financial targets achieved.

- The purpose of financial targets is to galvanize the operating units to manage performance and gain competencies for future success.

- It is one of many other perspectives but the one that funds the mission and purpose of the organization.

- It is a lagging indicator of performance because it records success after the fact.

Customer Perspective

What customer-centric objectives must be achieved to attain your strategic themes? This perspective is the second most forgotten or misunderstood set of objectives in business. Before setting goals using this perspective, answer the following questions:

- What is your target market?
- Who are/is your customer(s)?
- Who do they call our customers?
- Who do I compete against to gain the customer?
- What value does the existing customer of the organization perceive?
- If the organization disappeared, who would miss us? What will they do?

Often, the customers of today may not be the desired customers of tomorrow. As the audience of customers mature, what they desire in the organization changes also. What do your customers value?

Value, a term constantly used by marketing and business people, means many things to many people even as a definition. For the sake of fast learning, let us define *value proposition*:

> Value proposition is the emotional, physical and symbolic residue derived by a customer once this individual or organization purchases the product or service for a price.

A more detailed discussion of value and its major characteristics will be covered in Chapter 4 in relationship strategy, mission, and vision.

Often, the customer perspective is viewed as the set of objectives the organization must achieve to gain customer acquisition, acceptance, and perpetuation. These objectives are bounded or framed by the questions just listed. Objectives are an outgrowth of assumptions made about the customers and their habits, the markets they represent, and the value they perceive in a relationship with your organization.

Internal Perspective

Companies seldom fail because they have a wrong strategy. They fail because they lack the methods to achieve the tactics that surround a strategy. The internal perspective reminds us that the background works, driven by objectives and goals, must be in place to ensure that the customer and financial objectives are achieved. Internal processes, mores, cultures, and procedures in all departments and business units support the value proposition to the target market segments. Typically, organizations have habits that are challenging to break or change in these perspectives. In other words, their internal behaviors will sabotage their ability to meet targets in the customer and the financial perspectives. These organizations must re-tool to win, and this perspective helps them define what this retooling is. Conversely, if an organization can identify these internal characteristics and define ways to enable them, their execution arsenal can be tuned to win the customer and also destroy the competition.

Learning and Growth Perspective

Often laid-off before people, training and development is the first to be removed from any shrinking budget. In crisis, the furthering of the capabilities of an organization is usually sacrificed. Throughout history, organizations have behaved in short-term fashion, shrinking when times are tough and growing indiscriminately when times get better. This "inhale-exhale" methodology is what the learning and growth perspective serves to guard against. This perspective is the basis for all other perspectives and serves to remind the practitioner that the basis for all other results in the internal, customer, and financial perspectives is found in the learning and growth of the people. Learning, however, is not dictated by how you teach but by how people absorb new ideas and turn them into action. In a sense, it is more that just learning to action but the speed at which learning is transformed to action—a mean time between learning to action measure, so to speak. Often forgotten in strategy-delivery systems, *learning and growth* form the foundation for the capabilities of the organization. Usually, current failure in the competitive business world is the result of past failures in the acknowledgment and exploitation of learning and the growth of talent.

Examples of learning and growth issues include the following:

- Training and development of key managers and would-be managers in certain skills
- Access to information among teams within various silos of the organization
- Employee satisfaction and motivation measures

Learning and growth, under this definition, is not the indeterminate activities found in various organizations. This is measurable and linked to

IN THE REAL WORLD

The Learning and Growth Perspective in Action

Starbucks Corporation is hiring 200 employees per day[a] and building four stores per day[b] as well. This phenomenal growth could not have been achieved without the key ingredient of people. Employees at Starbucks strive to make their products—primarily, gourmet coffee—taste identical anywhere customers visit.

This cannot be achieved without an enormous amount of training and development of its people. How did this strategic imperative to winning ever happen? Fundamentally, its founder, Chairman and Chief Strategist Howard Schultz, built this value proposition into the fabric of his founding the company when he stated that Starbucks is about more than coffee but about people selling coffee to other people. He knew that the competitive advantage of his brand is found in the "equity of his people," and Starbucks developed their skills and provided them the environment to be the best they can be. He introduced benefits to part-time workers in his stores. He visits stores even today. He seems available to everyone in his company and has found that the secret weapon for the business: People come to Starbucks for the experience as much as for the coffee. It seems that Starbucks has based its strategy on the learning and growth of the team but has also not forgotten that it must balance all other perspectives in order to gain market share. Starbucks has also recognized the value of learning and growth as a strategic theme and has created a unique recipe of activities that "has linked to a unique relationship with their people (employees). Those people are linked to a unique relationship to the customers."[c]

[a] "Not a Johnny-Come-Latte," *USA Today* (September 9, 2003), p. 3B.
[b] Rob Howe," At Starbucks, the Future Is in Plastic," *Business 2.0* (August 2003), pp. 56–57.
[c] "Not a Johnny-Come-Latte," *USA Today* (September 9, 2003), p. 3B.

the other productivity measures. In other words, this learning and growth measures for objectives are aligned to key deliverables in the other perspectives. Furthermore, this perspective reminds us of the relevance of continued learning and growth goals and how they affect the continued competitiveness of the organization.

Understanding Cause and Effect: Strategy Mapping

When trying to understand anything complex, we tend to break ideas into their contributing parts. In computer science, the breaking of tasks down to smaller compositions is called *structured decomposition*. This is how computer programs are still written today. At Intel corporation, for example, complex tasks are broken down into objectives and key results so that every team member can understand the things to do, their owners, and what the results of the objectives are.

With Balanced Scorecard, the art of understanding the relationship among all key perspectives is done using *strategy mapping*—a technique of drawing the intricate relationships of cause and effect among all perspectives and their contributing parts. First, consider the following perspectives articulated in Exhibit 2.3.

The perspectives in Exhibit 2.3 illustrate a list of goals or strategic themes for a for-profit emerging organization serving the utility industry, but what seems to be missing is the cause and effects in these themes. The strategy map of Exhibit 2.3 is shown in Exhibit 2.4. Here, cause and effect has been linked using arrows that illustrate that each action or theme is dependent on another theme being executed. This seemingly simple exercise can be challenging because not all causes and effects are understood or communicated. Taking a large organization apart like this can be excruciatingly difficult, and the art is to keep it simple but accurate.

Generally, CEOs and their management teams are prone to state the main objectives in a form such as this: "Be and be perceived as the leader is the semiconductor industry." They leave the rest to translation. The

EXHIBIT 2.3

Sample Goals Using Four Perspectives

Financial Perspective

Achieve $250 million in new product revenue.

Achieve 60 percent margins.

Customer Perspective

Develop lead list of > 800/month.

Win new business in utility industry segment.

Attain 45 percent subscription-based business.

Internal Perspective

Drive utility market's specific needs into products once every year.

Develop sales channel for utility-based customers.

Lay off 5 percent of work force.

Learning and Growth Perspective

Build team that has utility experience in selling.

Develop and execute on-the-job training for all key employees on utilities.

---

problem with this method is that the translation of the key driving strategic thrusts/themes that can actually achieve the goal are seldom mapped or identified as a relationship map.

Reasons behind the Methodology

For organizations to be effective in operational potency, complexity and interrelationships between operational units must be understood and articulated. Similarly, these organizations must master the interrelationships between strategic intentions and the underlying operations actions that enable these intentions.

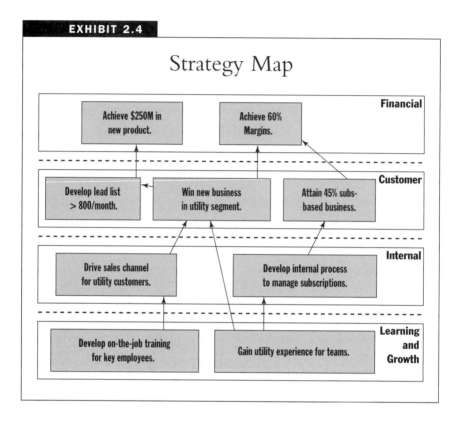

As illustrated in Exhibit 2.4, strategic mapping provides a visual framework for this operational translation, with an added bonus of illustrating cause and effect. In other words, the financial goals are usually caused by other actions within the customer, internal and learning and growth thrusts. The map draws on four or more perspectives that remind the organization of the key elements to operational effectiveness and strategy translation. It also shows the relationships (by the arrows) that documents the hierarchy or network of influences and dependencies to strategy achievement. This framework can be adjusted regularly and updated if strategic variables change. The ability to adjust such a map and

TIPS & TECHNIQUES

Clayton Christensen and Michael Raynor articulate a very important distinction between co-relation and cause and effect in their most recent article, "Why Hard-nosed Executives Should Care about Management Theory."[a] The article declares that many theories assume a cause-and-effect that is inaccurate because the assumptions lack the rigor of analysis. In developing strategy maps, this could be a very challenging opportunity, as it would really be natural to fall prey to the co-relationships and assume these relationships are truly cause and effect.

In viewing maps, consider the following before assigning cause and effect:

- Instead of studying why things succeed, learn why they can fail uncovering the necessary and sufficient conditions for success.

- Observation has significant power in understanding cause and effect. Attempt to ask key people the reasons for past performance.

- Get academics and consultants to assist you in this new skill development and make them aware of the need to uncover true cause and effect.

- Don't let the simplicity of display of the strategic map delude you into believing that the exercise is simple. It demands significant complex thinking to create simplicity.

- Understand the mechanism that causes an event, not just the relationship between the attribute of an event and the cause.

[a]Clayton M. Christensen and Michael E. Raynor, "Why Hard-nosed Executives Should Care about Management Theory," *Harvard Business Review* (September 2003).

to consequently adjust the strategic thrusts creates a resilient organization able to change and adapt as the stated goals are challenged by both internal and external forces.

Making BSC Work

Making BSC work generally requires the following steps:

1. Identify the purpose of the organization with mission, vision, and values.

2. Clarify strategy with an eye to competencies the organization has or can attain.

3. Break strategy into key themes that the organization can absorb.

4. Draw on strategy maps to understand cause-and-effect relationships between four-plus perspectives.

5. Develop performance measures within each perspective but also between perspectives, showing a balance of measures as well.

6. Build key scorecards around each objective and sub-objectives and initiatives.

7. Cascade theses objectives and initiatives with mutually organized measures to all levels of the organization to be used, shared, and evaluated on regular intervals.

Summary

Balanced Scorecard is a framework designed by Professor Robert Kaplan and David Norton. As the name implies, Balanced Scorecard is a methodology to solve challenges in balancing the multiple perspectives demanded of strategy with its execution. In a nutshell, BSC is a methodology for translating strategy into action. It has the following characteristics:

- Its methodology is suited for managing business strategy.

- It uses a common language at all levels of the organization.

- It uses a common set of principles to manage day-to-day operations as well as to framework the company's strategy.

- It is designed to identify and manage business purposes.
- It provides a balance between relatively opposing forces in strategy:
  - Between internal and external influences
  - Between leading and lagging indicators and measures
  - Between financial and nonfinancial goals
  - Between organizational silos focused on their own goals and an overarching framework of goals
  - Between finance priorities and operations
- It aligns strategic goals with objectives, targets, and metrics.
- It cascades to all levels of the organization.

The framework digests strategy but also focuses strategy into four perspectives of objectives. These perspectives may contain more than one strategic theme, and each theme is measured using performance measures. Each theme is also related to the others by cause and effect. This is the beauty of BSC, as it highlights cause and effect using a strategy map, a pictorial description of strategy and the relationships between the various perspectives.

CHAPTER 3

From Management to Performance Management

After reading this chapter, you will be able to

- Understand why information is no longer power.

- Understand what data obesity and knowledge starvation are.

- Understand the nature of information and its behavior. What brings relevance to information?

- Understand the ecosystem that feeds a Balanced Scorecard.

- Understand what performance measures are and what their types are.

- Understand the differences between leading and lagging indicators.

- Understand the relationship between co-related and non–co-related indicators.

- Understand the main perspectives in BSC; namely, financial, customer, internal, and learning and growth.

- Understand what targets, measures, initiatives, and objectives are.

Chris Meyer, author of *Fast Cycle Time* and *Blur*, says, "Marketing tracks market share, operations watches inventory, finance monitors costs and so on. Such results measures tell an organization where it stands in its effort to achieve goals but not how it got there or, even more important, what it should do differently."[1]

It is estimated that only 3 to 5 percent of corporate information is analyzed. Why is this not a surprise? Watch any business in the 2000s and note that executives are inundated with faxes, electronic mail, telephone messages, conference proceedings, direct mail, telemarketing calls, paper mail, and reports. In fact, if they actually read and analyzed everything they received, they would not do anything productive to improve the organizations. Just when executives thought they had control over information, the Internet revolutionized information accessibility and is transforming the very way in which business is performed. Now executives find themselves "surfing" for hours through the World Wide Web, setting triggers and agents to trap information swimming past their keyboards.

Business is not getting any more manageable. With corporate intranets, extranets, and knowledge network technologies entering the information management landscape in the Global 100, corporations will never die from starvation when it comes to information. They might die from indigestion. Too much and too fast, data with no analytical framework and no action seem, in fact, to be leading to *knowledge starvation* and *data obesity*.

Answering yes to more than two of the following questions signals that your company is suffering from data obesity and knowledge starvation:

- Do you go to a limited number of sources for information, or do you have to send out a search party? If you cannot get information readily, this is *data disintegration*.

- When you receive information, does it require that you reprocess it before it is applicable? If it must be altered before it is useful for performance measurements, it is *context insensitive information*.

- Is information lacking in timeliness and credibility? If so, it does not have *fitness of sources*.

- Does the information you receive force new questions? This is *depth of information*. Good business analytics really gets you to ask the right questions rather than move toward answering the wrong questions.

- Does the information lack dimensional views and perspectives? The information should allow the company to target products and services to customer A and channel B, for example. This quality is *data dimensionality*.

- Do you find that your organization gives you information that is at least one quarter too late? This shows a lack of *timeliness*.

- Have you not sent out information to test its value, and found that no one missed it? This shows a lack of *data usefulness*.

Obviously, then, information is not always viewed as an asset in organizations. Recently, the push for more and more information is having some negative effects:

- *The value of information diminishes with time.* Old, untimely information can be extremely destructive to the natural flow of business. Assumptions are made with data, and these assumptions could halt the successful momentum of a company's actions on products and services.

- *Information may have negative value when it is not only untimely but also wrong.* "Misinformation subtracts value from the valuable."[2] Wrong or outdated information may lead you to the wrong conclusions.

- *The value of information is relationship dependent.* That is, finite data are useless without the correct context and the relationship of the finite data to other finite data. For example, knowing about cost overruns in your factory is relevant, but it is more relevant when you can understand where and what caused them.

In a nutshell, information that is unused, updated, and unrelated is a depreciating asset and can turn into a liability very quickly.

New Frontier of Competitiveness

In the past, business enjoyed increasing market share and profits abounded. With the global competitiveness splitting the market pies, these companies are fast realizing that they must do more with what talent and tools they have.

In the search for the ultimate "magic pill," be it operational efficiency, gaining loyal customers, building a new mouse trap, or establishing a powerful value chain of vendors and suppliers, companies have discovered that the true lasting competitive advantage is not just the above-mentioned strategic themes but knowledge. Knowledge has long since been the theme song of the management gurus of the past century. But knowing without doing can be a waste of time and energy.

Beyond this discovery, the Global 100 is fast realizing that *self-knowledge* and applied self-knowledge is true power—that is, knowing yourself better than your competitor knows you, to act on your strengths effectively in your market space. For example, Wal-Mart changed the way manufacturers, brokers, retailers, and wholesalers performed work. It changed the entire business model and activities in the food industry. Knowing what it did well and knowing what its competitors did not know about the consumer brought Wal-Mart to victory with a 3 percent profit margin in the same businesses in which its competitors enjoy a less than 1 percent margin.

Winning in the food industry, which is a $500 billion business, Wal-Mart has triggered the industry into a cost-cutting efficiency adventure that will remove $30 billion in cost of the next five years. Wal-Mart used its self-knowledge and applied it for customer retention. More than information technology, Wal-Mart understands how to get the best from its technology and its vendors and its customers better than some others do.

We Need to Listen to "Moore"?

Gordon Moore, co-founder of Intel Corporation, introduced the notion of complexity growth when he declared that the microprocessor would double in complexity every two years.[3] The prediction has borne out to be a fact. It is believed that in the years to come, more power will exist in a single desktop computer than is the equivalent of all the computer power combined in our world today. Similarly, it is believed conservatively that the amount of private and corporate data stored on computers is doubling every twelve to eighteen months. Clearly, it is not a lack of information that holds corporations back.

Neither is it information technology. Faye Borthick, professor of accounting at Georgia State University, and Harold Roth, professor of accounting at the University of Tennessee in Knoxville, declare that "For the first time, information technology is sufficiently well developed that accountants can have the information they want."[4]

With the introduction of data warehousing, data-marting, data-mining, online analytical processing, three-tier client-server technologies, desktop navigation tools, search engines and hardware technologies, information technology seems to have popped up like intelligent mushrooms waiting to consume data and expel it to anyone at anytime and anywhere. These technologies, coupled with all the information overload, will only bring irrelevant data to us faster. Winning companies don't win by mastering quick access to information; they master the ability to, at a sustainable level, provide relevant information to the right people at the right time for the right managerial decision.

Peter Drucker stated that what is important is not tools. It is the concepts behind them that are important.[5] He declared that a conceptual map is sadly lacking in today's information to give it relevance to the decision maker. In some ways, the technological treadmill is going faster and faster, almost outstripping the needs of business and creating a life of its own.[6] This new market demand for executives to be powered by information to win gives birth to the knowledge leader, one who drives his business using analytical information as guide. The knowledge leader must now understand the fundamental competitive capability using these new-found tools is not how much information is gathered but how to optimize the mean time between decisions (MTBD). The leader must improve how fast the company can turn data into decisions to create a new landscape for its competitors to chart or it will be lost in the maze of information.

Information Is No Longer Power

Today, the knowledge leader cannot be measured by what information is obtained and dispensed but by what information is rejected, which will be significantly more. Without keen selection capability, the knowledge leader will be crushed under the sheer weight and demand of decisions to be made. Consequently, organizations that master the ability to understand themselves enough to make decisions, and command themselves enough to act decisively and consistently, will win. Information seems powerless. Decisive action using relevant information is power. Competitive advantage is best developed in the acquisition and deployment of relevant information to all who need and decide/act with it. What used to be in the careful hands of business analysts will shift dramatically to all managers and decision makers. There is no longer time for hierarchical decision-making protocols, only time for the hierarchy to hold the old bones of the corporation in place while the nervous system of the company fights the real wars of wealth acquisition. Relevant data are the fuel for this activity.

What Brings Relevance to Information?

Peter F. Drucker, the father of modern management, in his seminal article titled "The Information Executives Truly Need" contends that information should challenge basic assumptions and have links to strategy. He declares that BSC is such information.

Drucker states that enterprises are paid to create wealth, not control costs. But this premise is not reflected in traditional measurements. First-year accounting students are taught that the "balance sheet portrays the liquidation value of the enterprise and provides creditors with worst case information. But enterprises are not normally run to be liquidated."[7]

Drucker seems to believe that information is used for wealth creation. He breaks up information value into four main value categories:

1. *Foundation information.* Diagnostic, cash flow

2. *Productivity information.* Resource productivity

3. *Competence information.* Measure of the unique ability that customers pay for

4. *Resource-allocation information.* Managing scarce resources for the current business

Note that he believes these categories to be information on the current business condition and hence tactical in nature. BSC practitioners will declare that the greatest impediment to projects is the lack of upper management support. Upper management prefers strategy but must see the relationship between strategy and a strategy framework for the entire organization before supporting a BSC project. The questions surrounding the relationship of BSC to strategy will be discussed in Chapter 4.

Simply put, many organizations today are running forward while looking backward. These companies are blind to the strategic relationships among their true product value, their profitability, and their channel behavior. They lack the most basic of intelligence systems even to answer the more basic questions like, "Are the cycle time for your products and your cost of product creation co-related?" That is, do they track with one another? If so, what are the drivers of product demand and profit?

John Whitney, professor of Management at Columbia University and author of "Strategic Renewal for Business Units,"[8] hit the nail on the head when he said, "Indeed, I have found that perhaps most businesses do not know the true accrual profit of their products and services, and fewer still know the profitability of customers." BSC provides a relationship between strategic themes and the work performed or the key activities that organizations can affect.

In the commercial sector, information is used to uncover these issues but in the public sector, profitability is of no relevance. Budgets take precedence. Here the information circles around the question, "Do we have the resources to achieve the mission?" or "What are the key strategic goals with measures to achieve the mission?"

Relevance Is Subjective

Essentially, relevance is in the eyes of the beholder. Ultimately, decision makers at the strategic, operational and financial corners of an organization need information relevant to the decisions they must make. Morris Treadway of PricewaterhouseCoopers LLP describes relevance as "data suitable for a user's need."[9] This might sound anticlimactic, but let's explore this point further. In a nutshell, we know that any relevant information performance measurement must

- Link to strategy
- Be linked to activities and groups of activities
- Measure the loss of not doing
- Support the four main categories of Drucker's value model
- Feed and support an underlying concept

Performance Measurement: Down to Basics

In a study conducted by Will Schiemann & Associates, 97 percent of what they called *measurement-managed companies* talked of success in their change efforts.[10] We had discussed that the true measure of strategy is successful implementation of the goals and the achievements. But intermediary operational measures are necessary as a check and balance prior to the result, which might be more long term. In managing executive teams, measuring by the year will cause slippage year-to-year; measurement by the month will cause slippage month-to-month. In other words, the frequency of review is as important as the measure.

Measurement has had a bad reputation among the ranks because it only means that people get fired or demoted based on performance. However, measurement can be very valuable function in organizations whose people look for accountability. Many organizations lack the conviction to institute measurement for fear of a culture clash, that is, unhappy employees. But in further assessment, these organizations have found that a lack of measurement only allows the weak players to exist which further demoralizes the strong players who eventually leave the organization. Measurement without management is dangerous as it only becomes a static event. Management can transform measurement into a motivating force by using measurement as

- A gauge of performance rather than a tool for punishment
- A reward system
- A scorecard for learning and growth
- An anticipatory tool to analyze future events and prepare for them
- A tool for communicating priorities and what is important to the organization

Balanced Scorecard needs performance measurement. The result of a BSC exercise is a set of objectives with owners, measures, targets, and initiatives. As stated before, the hierarchy of relationships looks like this:

1. Vision

2. Mission

3. Values

4. Strategy and strategic thrusts/themes

5. Strategy mapping with perspectives

6. Objectives

7. Measures, targets, owners and initiatives

Given this hierarchy for the process, our next phase of discussion is performance measures within each perspective.

Exhibit 3.1 illustrates a perspective with an objective, measure, and target. Note that a customer perspective has been used as an example. In this exhibit, the following terms need to be addressed:

- Objective
- Measure
- Target

EXHIBIT 3.1

Sample Objective, Measures, and Targets

Strategic Theme 1

Children are healthy.

Objective 1

Pregnant women receive adequate care.

Performance Measures

- Percent of low income women receiving prenatal care in the first month of pregnancy

    TARGET > x%

- Percent of clients completing alcohol or drug treatment and are not abusing

    TARGET > y%

An *objective* is a goal to be achieved. In combination with other objectives, if achieved, it can achieve a strategic thrust.

A *measure* is a quantifiable formula whose variables define what needs to be measured and monitored in order that a target is achieved. For example, one measures the number of customers who were contacted or the amount of dollars spent on training. The example of a measure could be the number of customers with greater than 95 percent satisfaction.

A *target* is usually a numeric value to be achieved. It is a desired result of an objective executed. For example, an objective can have a target of 80 percent of customers with 95 percent satisfaction rating.

An *initiative* is a program, an activity, or a project that will meet an objective alone or in a combination with other initiatives. In the previous example, the initiatives that are launched must be accomplished to ensure that the objective is achieved. In this case, the initiatives look like this:

- Establish a customer satisfaction survey capability by February 2004.
- Deliver assessment at point-of-service.
- Ensure department follows up to achieve 60 percent.

Types of Measures

Measures can be one of four types:

1. Output measures

2. Input measures

3. Outcome measures

4. Feedback measures

Output Measures

Output measures are numeric output of an activity. Consider an activity titled "selling." The number of sales calls is an example of the output measure of the selling activity. Another example of an output measure is the number of demonstrations with respect to sales. In engineering, the number of bugs collected in a quality-testing evaluation could be an output measure.

Input Measures

Time and percentage of time are examples of *input measures*. Budgets or monies allocated to any activity are another example. Let's use the same example of "selling." A sales team can now understand the percent of time spent with selling customer A, customer B, and so on. In another sense, this team can measure the cost of the total activity of selling and/or the cost of selling customer A or B.

Outcome Measures

You might have met with the customer 100 times, but has the customer purchased your product? *Outcome measures* ask if the desired result of an activity has been achieved. Some nonprofit or government agencies have output measures that lack outcome measures. For example, a relief agency measured the number of times it assisted the needy in underdeveloped countries, and the number was very impressive. Further investigation revealed that many teams landed with little to no medical supplies. Furthermore, whenever they had supplies, looters and thugs stole these supplies. In this case, an output measure of the number of visits, combined with an outcome measure of the number of people saved with delivered medication, may work to understand the challenges.

Feedback Measures

A *feedback measure* is seldom discussed, but this measure has inherent value to a long-drawn process or activity. If chosen carefully, feedback measures help you gauge the quality of your output before an outcome appears. For example, software engineering processes can be rather complicated exercises, especially when engineers are developing code rapidly within teams. Testing these large amounts of software code is even more challenging, given the short time horizons. When testing begins, general experience indicates that the bugs cured or removed may seem to generate stable software.

One example is when my engineering team developed a measure of bugs called *weighted-defect count*. They measured the relative value of the bug and the number of them as an equation. When the weighted defect count went down, we may have been getting better but the outcome may not have been stable code. This is because we had a few bugs that were show-stoppers in the count that could stop the programs from performing at all. Hence, the team used a feedback measure of "# of level 1 bugs" just to measure the progress of removing the high-priority fatal bugs out of the system.

Leading and Lagging Indicators

Leading indicators are really drivers of performance. They drive the behavior of an activity, program, or process. If you measure the number of times we visit a client, that is an input measure and also one of many leading indicators of success. As they say, "Showing up is half the battle." A leading indicator of the economic potential in the high-tech industry is the book-to-bill ratio in the semiconductor industry. If the book-to-bill ratio is increasing, the market is in an upturn. This further indicates that if chip sales are up and growing, computer sales and retail sales will follow and hence drive the entire industry to a possible upturn. Thus, this ratio could be classified as a leading indicator. However, if you are in the semiconductor industry, the book-to-bill ratio may be a lagging indicator. You may have to find other leading indicators within your industry.

Are Measures Co-Related or Non–Co-Related?

Many BSCs fail because they use a large number of performance measures to describe or measure the same objective. Many measures are

Criteria for Picking
Performance Measures

The most important decision a modeler or BSC champion can make is in the choice of measures and items to measure. Hence, before choosing, ask the questions:

- Is the measure a leading or lagging indicator of performance?
- What type of measure is it?
- Why is this measure important? What does it tell me?
- Is this a simple way to uncover performance of any activity?
- What other measures that I am measuring give me the same result in another form?
- Can I get this measure regularly and automatically, or do I have to find it manually?
- What drives this measure?
- Is this measure an equational measure—that is, does it need to be formulated using a formula? Or is it just a single number?

Furthermore, performance measures must fit the following simple criteria for selection:

- Easy to understand
- Data source integrity—must come from a reliable and repeatable source
- Cause-and-effect driven
- Frequency of change
- Bounded variable—not too unstable behavior
- Accurate
- Representative of reality
- Relevant to the objective and strategy

Each perspective will contain several strategic objectives within it. Each objective may contain several measures, targets, and owners within it. Each of these objectives may be cascaded throughout the corporation and have scorecards associated with it also. Exhibit 3.2 illustrates such a construct. Note that this example covers a corporate objective to win in a particular business sector and has cascaded into marketing and sales. Marketing further cascades to Marketing Communications objectives that still feed the overall strategic theme. Not only is the strategic alignment evident, the performance measures all line up to a corporate measure thus removing any random choices of measures throughout the corporation.

EXHIBIT 3.2

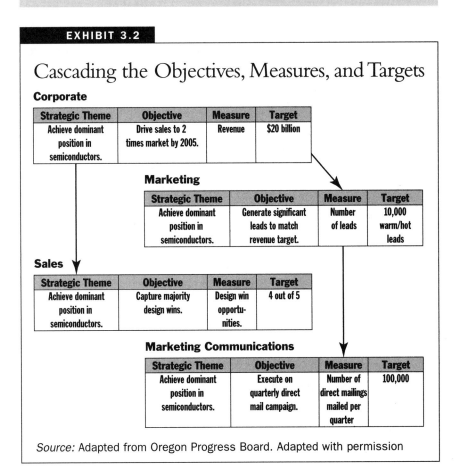

Cascading the Objectives, Measures, and Targets

Corporate

Strategic Theme	Objective	Measure	Target
Achieve dominant position in semiconductors.	Drive sales to 2 times market by 2005.	Revenue	$20 billion

Marketing

Strategic Theme	Objective	Measure	Target
Achieve dominant position in semiconductors.	Generate significant leads to match revenue target.	Number of leads	10,000 warm/hot leads

Sales

Strategic Theme	Objective	Measure	Target
Achieve dominant position in semiconductors.	Capture majority design wins.	Design win opportunities.	4 out of 5

Marketing Communications

Strategic Theme	Objective	Measure	Target
Achieve dominant position in semiconductors.	Execute on quarterly direct mail campaign.	Number of direct mailings mailed per quarter	100,000

Source: Adapted from Oregon Progress Board. Adapted with permission

inherently co-related—that is, they change in the same intervals. If one is building a measurement, monitoring, and management model of your strategy, co-relationship must be studied and understood. Why? In order to answer this question, first ask if the accuracy of the measure or the precision is more important. Many measures are accurate but not precise, and that might be okay. In another case, the reverse is true. If the viewer is less interested in the number than in whether the trends are up or down, correlated numbers need not be displayed or measured. If the numbers themselves are important and precision-oriented, then co-relationship might not matter.

For example, a sales organization can measure the number of sales orders as a lagging indicator of performance. But finance is measuring the number of purchase orders as a leading indicator for the production department. These are co-related drivers that show very little significance.

Are Measures Co-Related or Causal?

Just because measures interact with each other does not assume causality. Seventy percent of performance measures can be found in an organization. In some cases, many parts of an organization measure the same performance in different ways. Christopher D. Ittner and David Larcker, professors at the Wharton School, ask that you survey your databases and take inventory to clarify performance measures.[11] Furthermore, they recommend developing a *causal model* to isolate the performance drivers to achieving the strategic plan.

Keeping Perspective

Measures in the Customer Perspective

If the mission, values, and vision are the heart of an organization, the customers are the bloodstream that carries sustaining value to the organization. How customers are acquired and maintained are the main activities of a company. But the customer perspective measures the underlying goals/objectives that acquire, maintain, and grow customers. To understand measures in this area, one must first understand the following:

- Who is the ideal customer(s)?
- Can these customers be segmented by industries, tastes, expectations, age, agencies, function, business process, and so on?
- Who influences their buying behavior?
- Why do they buy—perceived and actual value/benefit of a purchase?
- When do they buy—budget cycles, timing of purchases?
- What do they buy—product issues, service, company image and positioning?
- How do they buy—are they trained to buy? What is their method of purchase?

The ultimate measurement of the success of a profit-centered organization is, "Did you sell something?" If the market buys, mistakes are forgiven. If it doesn't, they are not. Essentially, the binary nature of purchase or a vote, or an endorsement of a bill, is the ultimate measure.

But what are possible measures of the customer perspective? Given that we can set goals in this perspective that sets the tone for the key actions we take to ensure revenue, what would be the things we measure? To find a customer, *lead generation* would be an acceptable measure, namely, do we get 800 leads/quarter or don't we? These leads would be a lead indicator of revenue and a lag indicator of direct marketing campaigns. Retaining and evaluating customer satisfaction may demand satisfaction surveys. Research is indicating that just because your customers do not switch, one cannot assume that they are content. It just may be that they feel stuck with the solution that is offered. Hence, *satisfaction reviews* may be one measure while *customers attending user groups* could be another. The *percentage return business* is always a good measure of satisfaction.

Furthermore, buying customers may not indicate success when these customers could be buying more from your competitors. *Exclusive account control* could be another measure. Many measures are available. The art of measurement in the customer perspective is to identify key objectives that are derived from the main strategic thrusts as shown here:

A Strategic Thrust:

Win 50 percent market share in segment A by 2005

Customer Perspective Feeding This Could Be:

Be perceived as market leader in Technology B in segment A by 2003

Performance Measures Could Be:

- Percent market share in Technology B in segment B
- Percent satisfaction derived from survey results for 80 percent of installed base

Sample Customer Perspective Measures Are:

- Brand equity measures
- Market share
- Share of mind
- Total available market
- Total accessible market
- Customer retention
- Customer satisfaction
- Customer attrition
- Average selling price
- Lifetime value of customer

- Sales per employee
- Customer profitability by channel by product
- Design win (number of wins per year)

Measures in the Financial Perspective

Organizations are certainly not suffering from a lack of financial measures. Traditional measures still hold, but the relationship between goals, initiatives, targets, and measures is the new learning with Balanced Scorecard. Measures traditionally used in for-profit organizations to present the financial perspective include the following:

- Revenue
- Profit margin
- Gross margin
- Cost
- Cost of goods sold
- Cost of services
- Expense targets
- Risk adjusted return on capital
- Credit rating
- Debt rating
- Revenue per employee
- Return on X (e.g., equity, investment, assets)
- Cash flow
- Debt to equity ratio
- Earning before interest, taxes, depreciation, and amortization (EBITDA)
- Earnings

Nonprofit or government groups may use other measures:

- Budget shortfalls
- Expense targets
- Allocation from donors
- Allocation from legislatures
- Cost to deliver service
- Tax dollars/county

Measurement for the Internal Perspective

The internal perspective is associated with all the objectives and initiatives around the internal processes and capabilities of the organization. Hence, every measure from engineering productivity to manufacturing capability falls into this bucket. One should recognize that the common measure still prevails:

- Patents filed in engineering
- Product lifecycle measures:
  - Mean time between failures of existing products
  - Spec to prototype cycle
  - Bug-count on release
  - Weighted defect count
- Activity-based costs of major contributing activities and outputs
- Inventory turns
- Number of new products in pipeline
- R&D pipeline for new products
- Number of returns
- Percentage claims ratio (insurance company)

Measures in the Learning
and Growth Perspective

One of the greatest side effects of the BSC framework is the emphasis the Balanced Scorecard has placed on the fundamental participation of learning and growth in the cause-and-effect relationships. We can see that the learning and growth segment contributes to future capabilities of the organization and is rarely acknowledged and is usually the first to be cut in a tight market. Learning and growth measure examples are

- Training by level
- Retention numbers
- Redeployment percent
- Forced and unforced attrition
- One-on-one interviews per employee
- Employee and vendor satisfaction
- Pay benchmarks
- Rankings
- Six-month performance after hire
- Promotion from within
- Personal development plan creation

Targets

A target is usually a numeric value representing a desired result of an objective, goal, activity or initiative. Being a desired result, a target must have the following attributes:

- Attainable but a stretch
- Easily identifying and measurable
- Could be a single number or a formula

- Can be communicated to many leaders
- Have value if attained to a x-functional management team
- Linked to strategic variables
- Static and unchanging during the measurement period
- Benchmarkable with credible sources

Targets provide credibility to objectives and measures. One organization set the growth target to be two times industry growth. Note that industry growth is measurable and hence two times would fit the abovementioned criteria. Note also the target is static during the period and hence can be measured year after year.

Initiatives

These are programs and campaigns or projects that are launched to meet a target expectation. Objectives are sometimes high-level goals while initiatives ground these goals into necessary campaigns that need to be done in order to achieve the goals. An ISO-9000 initiative might be necessary to achieve manufacturing excellence for example. Initiatives display similar attributes to objectives such as these:

- Are attainable and can be measured
- Organization has the talent tools and time to perform them
- Is manageable within time expected
- Has an owner
- Is repeatable
- Is connected to the objective as a driver of the objective

Oregon "Shines" on Performance Measurement

In 2003, the director of State Government Operations, Gary Weeks, was tasked with making good on Governor Teodore Kulongowski's pledge to improve performance and accountability in Oregon state government. Gary convened a new Advisory Committee on Government Performance and Accountability in early 2003.

Alongside the Oregon Progress Board, an independent state planning and oversight agency created by the Legislature in 1989 (to keep Oregon focused on the 20-year strategic plan "Oregon Shines"), this advisory team was to establish guidelines for state agencies in linking performance measures to the Oregon Benchmarks.

The goal of this team is to continue the great work forged in the Oregon Strategic Plan formulated in 1989 and revised in 1997.

The Oregon Progress Board monitors the implementation of the plan and is chaired by the governor. The plan identifies the keys to progress in performance measurement system:[a]

- A unified vision
- Shared strategies
- Outcome-based evaluations
- Meaningful measures

Oregon state government has gained fame with Oregon Benchmarks, which is a set of gauges as to how Oregon is doing. The team is targeted to link Benchmarks to agency performance measures. Oregon has developed these measures in the 1999–01 budget:

- Eighteen benchmarks with two agencies
- Nineteen benchmarks with three agencies
- Eight benchmarks with four or more agencies

IN THE REAL WORLD CONTINUED

Now, Oregon is focused on bringing these common mission, and perspectives into an integrated measurement system. The expectations on these performance measures should include the following:

- Measures should gauge progress toward achieving agency goals and high-level outcomes.

- Measures should focus on the key indicators of agency success.

- Measures should have targets.

- Measures should use accurate and reliable data.

One of first issues tackled by the performance accountability team was the issue of multi-agency measures in child well being. Exhibit 3.3 shows a strategic map for this exercise with goals and objectives. This sample map does not include perspectives but is a map of cause-and-effect.

[a] Presentation by Jeff Tryens, Executive Director, Oregon Progress Board, to the Advisory Committee on Government Performance and Accountability (Performance Management Subcommittee) on May 27, 2003.

EXHIBIT 3.3

Strategy Map (Partial)—Child Well-Being

Source: Adapted from Oregon Progress Board. Adapted with permission.

Summary

Information is no longer power. Relevant information applied to action is power in corporations. Corporations are suffering from data obesity and information starvation. The symptoms were discussed.

The ecosystem that feeds a Balanced Scorecard is made up of vision, mission, values of the corporation; the competencies of the organization and the strategy. Without these preconditions, BSC cannot function well.

Performance measures and their nature were discussed. Output, outcome, and feedback measures were outlined and the between leading and lagging indicators; the relationship between co-related and non-co-related indicators were also explored. We introduced the four general perspectives of BSC:

1. Financial

2. Customer

3. Internal

4. Learning and growth

These perspectives form the balance in the scorecard, but it is not required that all four be represented. Nonprofits and mission-based organizations tend to include mission as the fifth perspective as an example.

CHAPTER 4

Mission, Vision, Values: The Precursor to Balanced Scorecard

After reading this chapter, you will be able to

- Understand what the many definitions of strategy are.
- Understand why strategy is important to BSC.
- Understand what the key elements of strategy are.
- Understand why strategy is not operational excellence.
- Understand what a mission is.
- Understand what vision is.
- Understand what values are.
- Understand why mission, vision, and values are important to BSC.

The CEO of a multibillion-dollar firm attended a presentation, from a certain consulting firm, about Balanced Scorecard. The consulting team, sponsored by internal vice presidents, presented the Balanced Scorecard framework with all its glory, connecting strategy to operational action, balancing key perspectives, and driving for key leading and lagging indicators.

Well prepared for the meeting, this CEO said, "I like the story, but don't you think we need to know our strategy, define our mission, values and vision before we embark on operationalizing this strategy?

That would mean we cannot do BSC before we satisfy the conditions to enable Balanced Scorecard."

What do you think? Should this CEO agree to continue the project, or should he ask for strategy work to commence?

Balanced Scorecard: The Digestive Tract of Strategy

Henry Mintzberg once stated the strategy is not the consequence of planning but the opposite, its starting point. He confirms what is instinctive in all leaders that to do, one must plan and to enable others to do, one must first create the playing field of action while bounding it with strategic intent.

Strategy cannot be left to interpretation. Many people have defined strategy as the things a corporation does to achieve goals; others have said that strategy is about staying fixed in a changing market. One can say the strategy is about positioning in the marketplace. They may be all right but still misplaced in their definitions. The essence of strategy is the science and art of devising plans to win over customers and other stakeholders.

Webster's[1] defines strategy as

- The science and art of employing the political, economic, psychological, and military forces of a nation or a group of nations to afford the maximum support to adopted policies in peace and war

- The science and art of military command executed to meet the enemy in combat under advantageous conditions

- A careful plan or method

- The art of devising or employing plans or stratagems toward a goal

Strategy is about engaging in battle with the enemy. Many people don't like the battle analogies, but in business this analogy does hold true.

When a for-profit business wins a customer, they take away revenue from other competitors and hence, destroy the economics of their competitors. This can be symbolic to battle. Strategy is the art and science of this economics driven to action plans. In strategy, corporations are using the art and science of exercising command and also employing all available resources for maximum support of policies and strategic themes. Strategy is about striking under advantageous conditions.

The essence of strategy is neither winning nor formulating to win. Under this description, strategy is about executing a plan or a set of plans. How does a corporation measure whether a strategic plan is a good one? Corporations can measure strategic themes in the following ways:

- Is it consistent?
- Does it address the needs of the stakeholders—that is, customers, shareholders, and employees?
- Does it affect the economics of the company positively?
- Does it affect the economics of key competitors negatively?
- Is it actionable?
- Does it have too many moving parts? Does it require too many conditions to be realized before it works?
- Are the assumptions consistent and within range of reason and bounded by real data?
- Does it have counter strategies built into the plan? What if the conditions are not satisfied?
- What if any one element of the strategy fails to be realized—is it fault tolerant?
- Is it easy to communicate?
- It may make you better, faster, and cheaper, but does it make you different?
- Is it a unique contribution to the marketplace?
- Does it gather an unfair percentage of the customers' perception of value?

- Is it time-dependent, or can it wait?
- Does it clarify the ideal customer target?
- Is it motivating with purposeful action?

How Is a Strategy Realized?

Frankly, a strategy cannot be divorced from its effective execution. One never knows until it is executed upon. Ironically, corporations are executing to a plan, daily. The question is, "Do we have a strategy behind it?" When employees at all levels of management wake up every morning and know why they are coming to work and what they have to do to advance the purpose of the organization, then strategy is realized. Strategy is not just about action but about focused action. This action is more about what is rejected as alternatives rather than about what is accomplished. For example, when a corporation is executing on a stated strategy, it is focused on who the ultimate customer target is, and it rejects anyone that does not fit the profile. It also chooses a strict direction in the market, battling only chosen competitors rather than anyone in their way.

Does Strategy Change When External Influences Change?

Given that we have just come through a major downturn in the high-technology industry, we cannot discount the effects of external factors to market dominance. However, the mark of great companies is the ability to anticipate external forces while building competencies that allow for the most advantageous conditions. It is really uphill when the best cyclists win. These winners had a plan and waited for the right time to move ahead. Similarly, great companies build a strategy in anticipation of situational influences that will affect others. Great companies are acyclic in their planning. They master the forces within their control and anticipate the effects of other external forces. However, they identify key strategic variables in their planning, and if these variables change in the marketplace, they reconstitute their strategy.

How Much Does Luck Play in Strategy?

It has been said that luck is the idol of the idle. Luck and timing are major factors in strategic success. But the assumption that strategy depends on luck is the wrong assumption. Strategy is a defined approach to the market, using the strengths and weaknesses of the markets and the corporation against the competitors in winning customers. Strategy is longer term than luck can anticipate. Execution depends on luck and timing, but strategy depends on longer-term elements. Howard Shultz, of Starbucks, decided that he was not just selling coffee but that Starbucks was about *people* selling coffee. Luck had nothing to do with this inspiring understanding of the market. After years of toil and trouble, this strategy is successful with epic proportions. It is found every time one engages with a Starbucks barrister—you can see strategy in action in their eyes.

Ralph Waldo Emerson once stated that shallow people believe in luck and in circumstances while strong people believe in cause and effect. Strategy combined with Balanced Scorecard trains and aligns the competencies within the corporation to uncover luck where it is hiding.

Essential Elements of Strategy

Sun Tzu states that if you know your enemy and yourself, then you can sustain a hundred battles. In that sense, the essential elements of strategy are as follows:

Know yourself
- Your unique attributes are displayed by what you do best.
- Your strategic positioning is displayed by where you fit in the marketplace in the minds of your customers and buyers.
- Know the value that stakeholders will pay for.

Know your enemy

- Understand their strengths and weaknesses
- Know where they are headed and how they plan to take on the market.
- Know how their leadership thinks.
- Know what they cannot change—that is, how they view their world, their personality, the unique way in which they interact with customers, the way they build products or services.

Know the customers

- Know what customers value disproportionately.
- Understand the segments and details of where your future buyers reside.
- Recognize that customers are not companies, they are people within these companies.
- Users of your product are not necessarily the ones who pay for the products.

Strategy Is Not Operational Excellence

Michael Porter, the guru of strategy and Harvard Business School professor, highlighted the very key differentiation between operational excellence and strategy.[2] In this article, he outlines that strategy:

- Is about positioning in target markets
- Is about being different and distinctive in the markets
- Is about delivering a unique value to customers
- Is about fit—which he defines as the unique combination of activities that define the corporate identity

He defines operational excellence about improving one activity while strategy is about orchestrating a set of activities in concert. Consider this analogy between operational excellence and strategy. Operational excellence is having the ingredients to a strategy while strategy is having a recipe for gaining differentiable operational potency.

Strategy as a Portfolio of Competencies

C. K. Prahalad and Gary Hamel, noted authors and thought leaders, declared that large businesses ran themselves as a portfolio of businesses rather than a portfolio of competencies. They articulated strategy as competencies and their exploitation. For example, Sony has a mission of building advanced technologies and innovation in the marketplace. Their competency seems to be in making electronics smaller—*miniaturization.*[3] Similarly, 3M Corporation makes many products, but what they have the capability to do best is adhesive products.[4] Strategy can be defined as the unique, differentiating value to the customer that is found in the personality and learned behaviors of the organization. In this definition, strategy can be the way the corporation builds and sells products and services. Identifying and exploiting these competencies is the challenge. New industries can be discovered if corporations can predict the competencies of future target markets and build them. Corporations that set out to identify future trends and isolate future necessitating competencies stand to win.

Competencies play a significant role in strategy formulation because they ground the planning phase with reality check. In strategy sessions, teams should ask themselves the following questions to ground themselves in the reality of their capabilities:

- Can we accomplish these grand dreams if we cannot execute them due to the unique skills and learning within the organization?
- Do we have to and can we acquire skills and learning to attend to the changing market demands?
- Who else can step up and deliver value with lasting competencies?

How to Identify, Isolate, and Exploit Core Competencies

Competencies come in two flavors:

1. *First-order competencies.* These are the set of skills and capabilities within the company that if organized well, provides a strong, competitive advantage in the marketplace. The recipe of this mix is key in delivering true value to the target customers. As an example, Southwest Airlines has isolated and exploited the key value proposition in their customers that the larger carriers essentially noted but did not serve. Customers wanted a way to fly short-hauls within the U.S. and not worry about losing bags and so on. They wanted to fly inexpensively but were willing to give up luxuries like food, and assigned seating. In return, they would like to get out on time and get to the destination on time. Southwest Airlines knew that flying was a hassle and that customers needed to know that a fun airline to fly did not mean that the airline did not take flying seriously. It is in this carefully constructed value proposition that Southwest airlines opened the skies to many non-flyers. (See In the Real World, "Taking Flight with Strategy.")

2. *Second-order competency.* This works in concert with the unique combination or recipe of activities that form the center of the value proposition to the customer. This competency is an overriding personality that an organization portrays to its customers and within. Consider Sony and how whatever they seem to do, they make things smaller. C. K. Prahalad and Gary Hamel describe this competency model extensively in their book titled *Competing for the Future.*[5]

The combination of both these defined competencies form the basis for whether strategy can be realized. Without capability and uniqueness in business design, strategy is nothing more than a word.

IN THE REAL WORLD

Taking Flight with Strategy

Southwest Airlines, a well-respected airline, originated in Texas to serve the short-haul markets. Now a strong player in the airline business, Southwest has learned to win with strategy. It chose specific strategic thrusts to drive its business forward. Although initially only directed tactically at "getting a plane in the air,"[a] Southwest has a far-reaching mission to provide inexpensive flights attempting to beat the larger carriers. It focused on key differentiating business architecture supported with financial attentiveness as seen in the following key competencies and activities that they wanted to dominate:

- Short-haul routes versus hub-spoke flights
- Kept the planes in the air with on-time, reliable departures (40 percent pilot utilization[b]).
- Flew only one form of aircraft Boeing 737s thus driving all training, learning, maintenance to streamlining and cost.
- Introduced profit sharing to all employees even before the union requested this.[c] With profit sharing came an attitude of cost conservation. There have been noted cases of SouthWest employees arguing on whether to spend more on items because they felt it was their profit that is being taken away.
- Celebrate everything they can in success, but don't spend too much money on parties.
- Low prices, but with acknowledged limited service in-flight and re-inventing seating requirements
- Strong humor in delivery of service

Above all, its belief systems have redefined air travel due to its focus on its delivery and its main cause "a symbol of freedom" as it alleviates the fear of flying with fun.

[a]Public presentation by COO Colleen Barrett, *Business Journal Power Breakfast*, Portland, Oregon, September 2003.
[b]James L. Heskett, Thomas O. Jones, Gary W. Loveman, W. Earl Sasser Jr., and Leonard A. Schlesinger, "Putting the Service Profit Chain to Work, Business Classics: 15 key concepts for Managerial Success," *Harvard Business Review*, pp. 110–120.
[c]Public presentation by COO Colleen Barrett, *Business Journal Power Breakfast*, Portland, Oregon, September 2003.

Mission Statements

Mission statements live in almost every organization. While strategy is the unique way an organization goes to market, mission defines the task at hand that the organization is assigned.

Southwest has a mission framed as "dedication to the highest quality of customer service delivered with a sense of warmth, friendliness, individual pride, and Company Spirit." Disney has a mission to make people happy. Often overused and trivialized, mission statements are critical to the execution or activation of strategy. As discussed before, strategy is the trigger for a Balanced Scorecard framework. Like coffee pours into a cup, BSC is the handle and framework that takes the key strategic thrusts, subcomponents of strategy, into a framework for management, monitoring, measuring, and direction setting.

Why Is a Mission Important to Balanced Scorecard?

Mission statements are not important to Balanced Scorecard as much as they are important to the drive of an organization. Missions are given to individuals and organizations. *Mission Impossible*, the old-time television series, used the phrase, "If you choose to accept this. . . ." Missions, by definition, have these characteristics:

- They are targeted and concise.
- They have strong emotional content.
- They must have meaning beyond the words on paper but in the action of the organization.
- They serve to define the objective of the organization.

The Texas State Auditors Office, which successfully performed Balanced Scorecard, states its mission as:

To actively provide government leaders with useful information that improves accountability.[6]

Qsent, a leading provider of contact information to businesses, states its mission as:

To perfect contact information[7]

What makes a mission worthy of attention and effective?

- Missions identify a reason for existing.
- Missions are tangible statements of organizational purpose.
- Missions declare the joint purpose between you and your stakeholders—namely, your employees, customers, shareholders, and sponsors.

IN THE REAL WORLD

Qsent Dials into Action-Based Values

Qsent, the accuracy leader, holds the following values and associated principles:

- *Customers define our success.* Customers are the focus of everything we do. Our first responsibility is to understand their needs and to provide quality products and services more promptly and dependably than our competitors.
- *Our people make it happen.* We treat each other with respect. People are encouraged to challenge, support, and participate with each other on adherence to our goals and plans. We innovate, work, and succeed as a team.
- *We value our commitments.* What we commit to, we deliver; what we are entrusted with, we protect.

Qsent has moved beyond value statements to cover operating principles to guide the organization. These underlying operating principles get to heart of how the organization can function using the values. Values are what the organization believes. Operating principles are how the organization acts on these beliefs.

Many for-profit organizations derive their mission statements as a key part of their organizational framework that includes a vision and a set of values.

Missions are essential part of the Balanced Scorecard for not-for-profit organizations and sometimes even replace the financial perspective as a higher-level guiding focus. The State of Texas Auditors Office defined its BSC perspectives to include mission attainment as the fifth perspective over and above all others because their financial goals were not the essential reason for being.[8]

They struggled to declare the financial perspective as paramount as a mission-centered organization. Essentially, the mission statement of any organization is a perspective, as it is the guiding focus of the organization's other perspectives and must be a balancing force to all other financial goals.

Southwest Airlines seems to have galvanized around its mission and has proven to be guided by very strong operating principles (see In The Real World in this chapter).

Values

As mission is why an organization exists, values are focused on how the organization will perform to the mission. *Values* guide the entire process of objective setting, goal acquisition, and strategy deployment. In fact, the key elements of mission, vision, and values drive the entire success of any organization. Recently, WorldCom and Enron, to mention just two of many, have put a bright light on the reason why values are important. Furthermore, these situations in publicly traded companies have shown the strong relationship between values and the valuation of companies. Arthur Andersen was a strong, vibrant accounting firm just a few years ago, and now it does not exist. Values—or the test of its values—made it extinct in a short period of time.

Organizations have taken value statements to heart and have found that any endeavor it performs is dependent on not just the end, but also the means to that end and values guide this value. It is not important how to derive value statements because many of the organizations contemplating Balanced Scorecard have stated values. It is, however, very important to ask the following questions about the relationship between values and scorecarding:

- Do your BSC objectives meet your values?
- How is your organization deploying BSC using the values as guide?
- Are there cases in which the needs of the few outweigh the needs of many, as in the case of layoffs? Is this a value contradiction?
- How does your organization view the values? Are they just stated and forgotten, or do you have examples of their use in business?
- Does your organization build alliances using values as guide?

In working with the U.S. Marine Corps, most of the work was built around an understanding of the mission and the values. Being a mission driven organization built on the purpose of making marines and winning battles, the U.S. Marine Corps tend not to work with organizations that do not share their value base. From a BSC perspective, values drive the way in which all activities surround the exercise, for example, how the team obtains information, how the team communicates, what is important in the perspectives, how to view learning and growth.

The USMCs values are:

- *Honor.* Integrity, responsibility, accountability
- *Courage.* Do the right thing, in the right way, for the right reasons
- *Commitment.* Devotion to the corps and my fellow marines

I ran an organization, built on values, and believe it to be the fundamental framework for work. It was tested everyday in the course of building the organization and was the basis for all managerial action and effectiveness:

- Respect
- Winning
- Making a difference

TIPS & TECHNIQUES

Moving from Values to Operating Principles

In the course of working with several organizations and operating units, one challenge arises around value statements. People don't seem to understand them or value them because they cannot identify them when they occur in companies and employees only remember the times when the values were violated in their presence. One way to ground value statements is to test your teams with the following expectations:

- Ask members of your team to outline how the values can be translated to action and record these action methods.
- Ask members to outline how they want to operate and structure the way that their values are turned into action, that is, how they will be expressing the values on a day-to-day basis.
- Start each exercise with the following frame of reference:
  - For example, *I would like to hold one-on-one meetings with each of the people in my team because I respect my team members.* Note that the operating principle leads the statement and the values end the statement, thus fusing the operating principle with the value that it expresses and exercises.
  - Make each team member talk through this exercise and consolidate all feedback into an organizational operating principle set with examples.

- Commitment to excellence
- Balance

We made all of our decisions based on these values even though they sometimes contradicted each other. All in all, values drive the how of business while the mission sets the target.

Vision

A vision is the dream that never leaves you. "Vision is a dream or picture of the future that draws us—no pulls us into the future."[9] It is the picture of what an organization believes the future can be. It details the world better for the use of the organizations tools, products, and services. Vision statements show everyone what the world can be.

Vision statements are

- Significantly motivating
- A selling document
- A communications tool used to solicit members and stakeholders
- A driving dream of the way things can be

Summary

What Are the Many Definitions of Strategy? Strategy has been defined in several ways, but the key descriptors of strategy are described by Michael Porter, C. K. Prahalad, Gary Hamel, and other thought leaders. They provide the methods of identifying unique positions in markets.

Why Is Strategy Important to BSC? Without strategy, organizations cannot isolate key strategic themes to pursue. Without strategic themes, organizations cannot formulate key perspectives to focus on themes. Without the key perspectives, BSC is not a balanced set of perspectives and the model will break down. BSC is the digestive tract with strategy as its food.

Strategic positioning in the marketplace that is the unique and differentiable set of activities that define an organization. This unique set of activities can come together as ingredients into a recipe. One can also consider that a key element of strategy is the core competency found within the hearts and minds of the corporation. High-order competency is an ability to administer key value to the customer that is unique—that is, the ability of Southwest to deliver on time, fun flight experiences.

What Are the Key Elements of Strategy? The key elements of strategy are:

- Know yourself
- Know your enemies
- Know your customers

Why Is Strategy Not Operational Excellence? Strategy is about doing activities differently in the marketplace while operational excellence is about doing different activities.

What Is a Mission?
- Missions identify a reason for existing.
- Missions are tangible statements of organizational purpose.
- Missions declare the joint purpose between you and your stakeholders namely your employees, your customers, your shareholders and yours sponsors.

What Is Vision? It is the picture of what an organization believes the future can be. It details the world better for the use of the organizations tools, products, and services. Vision statements show everyone what the world can be.

What Are Values? As mission is why an organization exists, values are focused on how the organization will perform to the mission. Values guide the entire process of objective setting, goal acquisition, and strategy deployment

Why Are Mission, Vision, and Values Important to BSC? Mission, vision, and values are the basis not just for BSC but for any actions a corporation will undertake. Without these statements of purpose, the guiding principles of a corporation will not exist. Guiding principles articulate for all concerned the personality of the corporation, and strategy is a reflection of that personality in action.

CHAPTER 5

Six Success Factors to Implementing Balanced Scorecard

After reading this chapter, you will be able to

- Understand the key success factors to implementing BSC.

- Understand that the success factors are a collection of virtues that do not guarantee success, but give organizations a guide to success.

- Understand that success factors are seldom found in one organization, but are a collection of factors found in several organizations that have succeeded not just in BSC, but in implementing other analytic applications and methods such as activity-based costing, total quality management, and the like.

- Understand the way these success factors work in concert with each other to enable a significant and sustainable BSC implementation.

The six success factors covered in this chapter are suggested methods that combine the success conditions identified by several organizations. This method is not a cookbook to success but a collection of conditions found in several successful BSC implementations. Ironically, the organizational challenges and implications encountered in implementing analytic methods like BSC require that implementers focus on three axes of considerations:

1. The people issues and challenges in change management

2. The process issues that require a removal or and addition of new processes to enable the transformation

3. The technology that sustains and enables the continuous improvement

Program initiatives like total quality management (TQM), activity-based cost/management (ABC/M), customer relationship management (CRM) and the like have taken these paths over the years, and the knowledge gained from these implementations is available for comparison to the BSC challenges. Many of the implementations secrets used in other analytic applications like ABC/M, TQM, and CRM are applicable to BSC implementation.

Exhibit 5.1 illustrates this combination of insights. Its premise is "knowing before doing; doing before showing." Note also that the

EXHIBIT 5.1

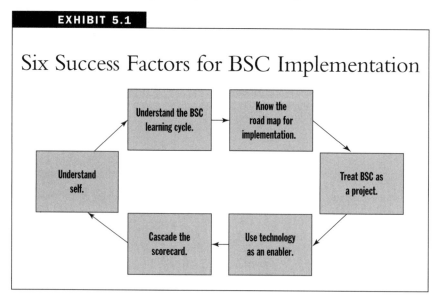

Six Success Factors for BSC Implementation

premise contends that organizations have little control over the outcome of a project; they might have control over establishing the preconditions of a successful implementation.

Success Factor One: Understand Self

Many organizations seek BSC to mobilize their strategy when they find difficulty expressing their strategy. Others join the BSC wagon to communicate strategy or to operationalize performance measures when they have a history of incapacity to make and stick to a decision. BSC cannot solve the problems that are found in the basic building blocks in an organization. John Lingle and William Schiemann, authors of the article "From Balanced Scorecard to Strategic Gauges; Is Measurement Worth It?" confirm that "To the extent that an organization, like an individual, must 'know thyself' to be effective, then executives face an urgent task of reexamining their measurement system to gain greater self-knowledge and self-confidence."[1] Furthermore, BSC will formalize any strategy, if consistent. It may not be designed to test the viability of the strategy. It will come close by providing a balanced view of the strategy and allow for more questions to be asked around measures and around the ability to mobilize through the organization. But if a company cannot understand its own capabilities or competencies, or has incapacitating habits, then BSC will not work. Pat Cox, CEO of Qsent, the accuracy leader in contact information management, understood his organization's absorption capabilities early and set about to adjust BSC to fit an emerging business mentality (see "In the Real World" in this chapter). The organization should know itself well enough to know what it is willing to do once armed with BSC information. Organizations have biases and have ways to solve problems. BSC can only succeed if it adapts to these biases and perspectives.

IN THE REAL WORLD

Qsent Keeps
Scorecards Simple

Qsent (*www.qsent.com*), the leader in accurate contact information, is embarking on Balanced Scorecard even though it is a venture-backed startup. Pat Cox, CEO of Qsent, emphasizes that the organization is facing high growth and needs a mechanism to scale its business strategy as well as share its strategy with every employee of the company.

This small startup, with big dreams, has attempted to build performance measurement into its fabric but this attempt did not take hold the first time. The market shifted in midstream, and it had to refocus not just on balance but also on delivering revenue and nothing else. This focus took it away from Balanced Scorecard for a year.

Now it is re-energizing its entire management team to deliver growing revenues in these tough times. For Qsent, Balanced Scorecard is the framework for delivering strategy to its employees and to communicate the value of their work.

Francisco Garbayo, senior vice-president of Human Resources, is leading the implementation. The Qsent board of directors, who have endorsed the process, looks to him and Pat for a cohesive method to motivate, measure, and manage the organization's growth cycle from startup to enterprise.

In a meeting on scorecarding, Pat's first instincts about BSC were that it seemed too complicated for digestion in an emerging company. He asked that the educational demands on the classic BSC would take too long and would be challenging for an emerging business so focused on the marketplace. However, he realized the value of a simpler model adjusted for emerging businesses, as he sees the need for the following:

● Moving strategy from top management to all employees

● Managing with the same goals across all his VPs

Success Factor Two: Understand the BSC Learning Cycle

Champions who lead BSC efforts are fast learners who expect others to move and be motivated by the same ideas and at the same speeds. Unfortunately, this is seldom the case in organizations. Furthermore, organizations learn and adopt new methodology differently. But there are some distinct phases that methodologies like BSC go through. These phases, once understood, can be enabled for fast organizational absorption or adoption. Understanding how they evolved in the phases will help organizations pace themselves and watch for the signs that permit them to move along in the phases.

Success Factor Three: Know the Road Map for Implementation

BSC implementation requires focused attention on the people, process, and technology fronts. Besides all the theory and real-world experience, this success factor is about what to do to drive the project. There is no magic in this success factor except for the significant activities that go into implementing the project using meetings, goals, and objectives, selection criteria for vendors and consultants, choice of champions and team members, and the attainment of support.

Success Factor Four: Treat BSC as a Project

Several successful BSC implementations have learned that the best way to make BSC a part of the business culture is to "projectize" and "productize" the endeavor. If organizations are product- and project-oriented, making the project have ship dates, product-freeze schedules, and product lifecycles only enhances the chances for use. Furthermore, treating the clients of the information as your customers forces a formalism for success.

Success Factor Five: Use Technology as an Enabler

Technology has come a long way in the years that BSC has been endorsed and implemented in organizations. Given the sophistication of these technologies, BSC implementations can take full advantage to accelerate the projects using technology as enabler. Three main technological frameworks exist in the market thus far:

1. Enterprisewide performance management systems

2. Stand-alone but integrated BSC systems or business intelligence systems

3. In-house custom-built BSC systems

All of these systems may seem different, but they can be viewed with a common framework for learning and implementation.

Success Factor Six: Cascade the Scorecard

Many team members are so excited about pilot programs that they charge like rhinos in a straight line and at high speed. Their passion drives them to work long and hard hours, demanding everything from everyone. They gather data through interviews and use hand-drawn process charts to accelerate the results. They finish the project and produce the finest reports in the history of the company. The project leader gets a large and heavy plaque for his or her cubicle and the celebration begins. The next morning, the CEO visits the champion in excitement and asks that the project be performed across the entire company and promotes the champion to director. But the CEO wants the results to be derived faster than before. In fact, now that it is mostly done anyway, the CEO wants reports monthly to analyze all 20 locations, starting three months from now. If the project does not consider all the elements to cascading BSC across multiple lines of business, multiple countries and cultures, the pilot project will fall in between the phases of pilot to production. The sixth success factor is the one that moves BSC from project ignition to a way of doing business. But there is a seventh success factor—an invisible factor—that is the foundation for all others. It is covered in Tips & Techniques, "Seventh Invisible Success Factor."

TIPS & TECHNIQUES

Seventh Invisible Success Factor

The number-one reason why BSC projects fail is lack of senior management support. Unfortunately, those that hold the purse pay the bills. This would be the obvious reason why programs fail. Nothing in this book will work if management does not support the necessity of the program. Frankly, nothing in this book will work if the organization *at all levels* does not support the program. In the end, the most successful companies are predisposed to the realization that change is necessary and also predisposed to acquiring the skills and competencies necessary to win with strategy. For that reason, the seventh and most important success factor—support—is not explored as a factor but as a fundamental spine of the entire book. But it is important to review how to get upper or senior management support:

- *Never assume support.*
  - Always sell the idea because management can forget rapidly the value proposition of BSC.

- Find the key influencers and influencers to the management teams and connect BSC to them.
- *Educate, educate, educate.*
  - Learning does turn into action, hence, give the teams constant information about successes and failures to prepare them for change.
  - Never assume that the information flow should be one way. Assemble meetings, both informal and formal, to awaken their (the users of BSC in the future) motivations.
  - Don't assume that the future users of BSC are rejecting the idea and are done with it. Sometimes, the method comes before the need. Let the team form its own ideas of the purpose and sometimes, they will discover the value of BSC given the right circumstances.
- *Don't position BSC as the reason for living.*
  - BSC is a means to an end and not the all-encompassing purpose for action.
  - Position BSC as one more tool in the toolbox for managers to communicate and articulate strategy.
  - Make it fun and make it an imperative.
- Ask whichever team is challenged with strategy what they can suggest to solve the challenges in strategy and let them back into BSC as a methodology.
- *Don't say "initiative," say "way of working."*
  - BSC can be a fad, and some team members may be hoping it is.
  - BSC must be positioned as a way of doing business, and this should be reflected in funding and resource allocation.
  - Be patient, even though time is our enemy. In changing a business practice, pushing too fast can destroy great events.

> **TIPS & TECHNIQUES CONTINUED**
>
> - *Let someone else more credible sell the story.*
>   - Consultants and academics can sell an idea better than internal advocates.
>   - Even if the CEO is selling the idea, the stigma associated with internal agendas and the like, can hold back progress.
>   - More often than not, the CEO can come back from a flight having read the latest book of Y and is pushing the idea. Organizations have learned to cope and protect against these syndromes however good they may be for them. Bringing in people who are convincing and carry a reputation for success can speed up the process of adoption.

Summary

There are six key success factors to implementing a BSC project:

1. Understand self

2. Understand the BSC learning cycle

3. Know the road map for implementation

4. Treat BSC as a project

5. Use technology as an enabler

6. Cascade the scorecard

Each of these success factors works in concert with one another to increase the possibility of a successful implementation.

Upper management support is essential and almost a seventh success factor, and the gathering of upper management support is discussed throughout the book rather than highlighted as a success factor.

CHAPTER 6

Success Factor One: Understand Self

After reading this chapter, you will be able to

- Understand how to identify your organizational readiness for change.
- Understand how to identify if your change leader's personality fits the task at hand.
- Recognize if the CEO and management team are ready to institutionalize BSC.
- Understand what task-relevant leadership is.
- Understand what task-relevant readiness is.
- Recognize what the three personalities of a change-ready organization are.

When executives ask me to assist with business transformation, it is usually after they see that the current method is not working. Organizations are more open to listening to new ideas when they are imprisoned by their current circumstance. But this does not guarantee a successful change implementation. Listening and commitment are only two of several factors.

Experience dictates a set of key questions to determine the probability of success in their new Balance Scorecard adventure:

- Have you or your organization/business unit created a transforming initiative from within your organization?

- Have you or your organization supported other initiatives that changed the business process of your business unit?

- Have you or your organization successfully implemented supporting technology for infrastructure, software, or systems that enable this new process?

- Have you or your organization led a business transformation initiative from start to pilot to enterprise deployment?

- Have you or your organization hired and managed external consultants to support a transformation team?

If your answer is yes to all of these questions, the probability of succeeding in your next business transformation is higher than if you said no to a majority of these questions. The best measure of future success is past performance in similar circumstances. However, organizations change anyway. They transform in competencies as business units transform in hiring, firing, and organizing.

Organizations frequently dive into BSC projects like eager children jumping into a swimming pool on a hot summer day. The enthusiasm can only be dwarfed by the utter lack of planning some organizations undertake in truly understanding the venture they embark upon.

The challenge many BSC teams take on is perceived as a change management challenge. Many of these teams are led by dynamic professionals who are determined to show a better way to their organizations. They are progressive, rule-changing, and intelligent change agents who see possibilities of change but are seldom accustomed to the politics of change. Many are rational-centered people, that is, they believe that logic and results speak for themselves; that truth will be understood when presented. This is unfortunately not always the case.

"There's no reason so many people are cynical of canned change programs and distrustful of the "change wienies" sent to administer them. It's the same reason so many change programs fail: They have nothing to do with what really matters in business."[1] The literature is not lacking from change management research and books. So let's not dwell too long on the ways to change and instigate change. However, the major aspect of this illustration is to recognize that no matter what the value of the information and experience, human perception can hold back a BSC project. And reality is still in the eyes of the beholder in business today. If you do not understand the way in which your company deals with truth and information, you will never get anywhere with new information. Many companies who have failed in several initiatives tend to believe that the next one will do the job. This naïve notion is more the root cause because it is the real reason why they fail—they lack an understanding of their incapacities and skills. Other companies succeed in their BSC initiatives because they have a strict culture for change and can make brash information system changes without reaction. Many times, understanding yourself and your organization's readiness to change determines your quotient for success. Let's call this *task-relevant readiness*.[2]

The readiness and context-maturity is the organization's ability to respond to and strive for outputs from a BSC project. On occasion, I have had the difficult task of counseling program managers who are about to launch their BSC projects. Almost all BSC-related conferences can educate them on what to avoid and how to make things great. Three main ingredients to ignition must be addressed:

1. *Transformation-relevant leadership.* Are the CEO and executive team ready to institute BSC?

2. *Task-relevant leadership.* Is the champion ready to lead?

3. *Task-relevant readiness.* Is the organization ready to follow?

Tranformation-Relevant Leadership: Are the CEO and Team Ready to Institute BSC?

Think whatever you want, but change starts from the top. Initiatives are started anywhere in an organization, but transformation is enabled from the executive offices. Whether organizations are top-down driven or middle-managed, the CEO and executive team make sustaining transformation happen. Mark Ganz, CEO of The Regence Group, transformed his organization from one focused on wholesale to retail purely by setting the tone and the example for change. He instituted a series of team meetings that he attended personally for three days a week for nine weeks. His presence and participation drove the seriousness of the cause.

Usually, BSC has begun from one department or from the top, but the keys to full deployment lie in the senior management. Senior management tends to assign the tasks of defining, implementing, and sustaining BSC using champions within the organization. But champions need to get the priorities of each stakeholder in perspective before starting the project (see Tips & Techniques, "Start with Questions of Priority").

TIPS & TECHNIQUES

Start with Questions of Priority

Ensure that the senior team is not just behind BSC, but that it is aligned in why BSC is being instituted. The lack of alignment between the key leaders can translate into a losing proposition from the start. Consider the priorities displayed in Exhibit 6.1 in which each team has the same ingredient expectations but in different priority order. Once the champion and team begin their project, they will be challenged with different deliverables by the CEO, the management team, and the task force. These mismatched priorities and purposes can be tested.

A simple test will align all priorities or at least make everyone aware of the discrepancies:

TIPS & TECHNIQUES CONTINUED

❶ Using Exhibit 6.1, interview the key management teams, members, and CEO.

❷ Ask them what they wish BSC to achieve for them and ask them to order these expectations in order of importance. What is the order of expected delivery?

❸ Publish the final report identifying these differences and explain how you will satisfy their expectations.

Exhibit 6.1 tells us that the BSC project will be challenged as there is a chance that mixed messages will be received by the company. If the CEO wants strategy communicated while the management team wants to reward and punish, the CEO will be viewed as inconsistent and the management team will be viewed as the assassinators of a culture.

If a transformation team ignores this discrepancy, it will look like agents of the prime directive—namely, the control of the people. The CEO wanted to motivate but the management team wanted to get tighter on its management process. One wanted motivated action while the other wanted measurement and punishment. This can be solved if communicated, as teams will align priorities and purpose once aware of inconsistencies and the project will flow well.

EXHIBIT 6.1

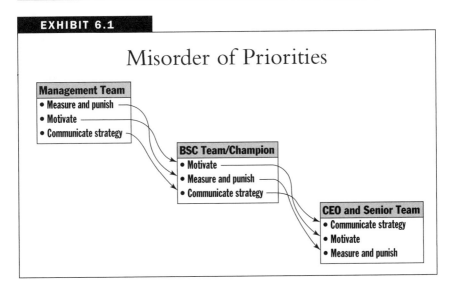

Misorder of Priorities

Management Team
- Measure and punish
- Motivate
- Communicate strategy

BSC Team/Champion
- Motivate
- Measure and punish
- Communicate strategy

CEO and Senior Team
- Communicate strategy
- Motivate
- Measure and punish

With BSC, they are probably charged with making strategy everyone's job. But many teams may have other primary priorities.

Task-Relevant Leadership: Is the Champion Ready to Lead?

Is the champion ready to lead a BSC program? Can the champion absorb this strong responsibility and ensure that it succeeds?

BSC pilot projects benefit a great deal from targeted, passionate leadership. Leaders of the projects often have a mission—that is, to improve and change the enterprise. If you lead or are about to lead a BSC project, you probably have a strong desire to change the way the business around you behaves. Generally, the typical BSC project is profiled as follows:

- Champion reports to the senior management of an organization.

- Finances are initiated but the goal is operational usage of information for decision making.

- BSC is steering committee driven. Most projects have an executive committee overseeing the activities of the program.

- There is powerful executive sponsorship.

- Most projects also use a cross-functional team to drive the program.

- Pilot off-the-shelf but connected software is used.

- An external consultant may be used. Other times internal consultants are engaged.

- Most teams are charged with a set of objectives.

- Most of these teams are looking for the "*Aha!*-effect," that is, looking to be surprised by their discovery instead of merely establishing a methodology in their organization.

Champions have distinct personalities. Apart from the risk-taking "do or die" mentality, champions

- Are visionaries and see the future bright with changes
- Have key skills that are relevant to BSC
- Have a larger awareness and broad perspective beyond any functional team
- Have established a mental plan and methodology to take the company from point A to point B

Traits of Successful BSC Leaders

Certain definite traits of successful BSC program leaders surface in the course of a BSC exercise:

- Renegades and nonconformists
- Enjoyment of "missionary" selling and are convincing in their communication skills
- Enjoyment of and demand for change
- Impatience with the way things are
- Rapid learners who enjoy knowledge above routine actions
- BSC knowledgeable
- Somewhat cynical about the way business is performed today
- Lonely in their mission and sometimes afraid that very few understand their goals
- Possessed with an eye for detail but with the big picture in their view
- Enjoyment with being visible to upper management
- Frustrated about limited resources on the project because the mission is above any other goal
- Believe that they need more support from management and that management ought to just order everyone to follow because it is so obvious
- A strong entrepreneurial spirit and associated skills to build a small company within a big one

- Belief that they cannot last long in the BSC program and will have to move on after
- Skilled communicators with IT groups, finance teams, and operational teams
- Enjoyment with getting past "bean counting" to work with the operational teams
- Ability to motivate volunteers or part-time assignees to the program
- Easily bored; likes movement
- Enjoyment in the rush of the new challenge
- Impatience with generally acceptable standards
- Impatience with routine procedures and policies; likes to get to the right answers
- Disinterest in repeatability, scalability, and maintainability
- Ability to get things done without asking permission but asking for forgiveness

Not all these skills and traits may be contained in one individual but may be shared among your team members.

Team Member Composition

Effective teams have key traits, also. The key to composing a BSC team is balance. Balancing the team with diverse skills is essential. As Jim Collins states, it is important to get the right people on the bus and on the right seats.[3] Several seats are crucial to a BSC implementation:

- A champion, leader
- A model creator, analyst
- A functional group representation or more
- A thought leader, methodology expert
- An academic/university research connection

Task-Relevant Readiness: Is the Organization Ready for BSC?

BSC usually begins as an initiative within most organizations. These firms want to analyze and change the way they view their business, their strategic implementation capabilities.

First, one of the most documented reasons why BSC projects fail is "the lack of upper management support." Nine out of ten case studies speak of this phenomenon. Although the best way to improve your chances of implementing BSC is to get management support, this borrowed authority and endorsement is only a smoke screen to a more systemic problem—the readiness of your organization to accept, embrace, and use new ideas and concepts for improvement.

Preparation for the BSC Journey

Before you embark on your BSC journey, try to understand and then plan through four aspects of readiness (see Exhibit 6.2):

EXHIBIT 6.2

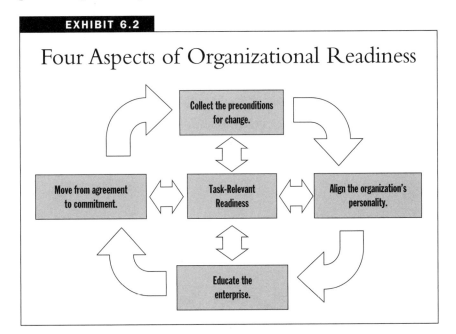

Four Aspects of Organizational Readiness

Collect the preconditions for change.

Move from agreement to commitment.

Task-Relevant Readiness

Align the organization's personality.

Educate the enterprise.

1. Collect the preconditions for change.

2. Align the organization's personality.

3. Educate the enterprise.

4. Move from agreement to commitment.

Collect the Key Ingredients to Project Ignition

Organizations are usually resisting change when change is the only way they can survive out of the situation at hand. Why should anyone be surprised that teams resist change? However, the true change-agent is attracted to resistance. Like metal to magnets, BSC leaders enjoy the challenge of change.

Organizations have similar yet contradicting profiles:

- *Change-fatigued—too tired of change programs.* Many just wish to wait it out until the CEO gets another idea. Some organizations actually enjoy anticipating change programs by the number of books the executive officers read.

- *Questioning the business value—too frustrated with quick fixes.* Many organizations will debate the value of any new methodology, especially when it means that resources have to be applied.

- *Observing who sponsors the program—weary of politics.* Organizations will watch where the wind blows and will tend to follow when they believe that there is no way out in the short term. One should not mistake agreement for commitment in BSC programs. BSC requires strong buy-in to work from the key change sponsors. The rest of the organization will transform by observing their commitment.

- *Measures and rewards—primary motivators.* "Measure me and I will move. Reward me and I will leap" seems to be today's business battle cry.

What we have discussed are the basic lowest common-denominator conditions in many organizations today. These conditions have to be understood and worked when performing a BSC exercise. Beyond the basics, these perspectives replace fear, uncertainty, and anxiety with momentum and commitment. Projects can go one of two ways—they can ignite or they can combust. Project ignition demands that the BSC champion bring the following preconditions into focus:

- *Vision.* The ability to see and articulate the way things can be
- *Knowledge.* The awareness built on keen, leading-edge thinking and analysis
- *Experience.* The practical, hands-on awareness derived from "being-there, doing-it"

All three of these preconditions if applied to the three main enablers in any BSC project—people, process, technology—can reduce risks and increase the probability of success (see Exhibit 6.3).

EXHIBIT 6.3

Aligning the Organizational Personality with Preconditions

	Vision	Knowledge	Experience
People	Executives, CEOs	Educators, thought leaders	Practitioners, BSC modelers, project leaders
Process	BSC cycle, project management, objectives setting and decision making expectations	Educators in the industry, consultants, modelers	Industry-specific examples, cases, best practices, worst practices
Technology	Chief information officers, BSC committee	Technology consultants, software vendors	Software vendors, IT department resources, user-group forums

BSC champions must identify the sources of these preconditions and apply all these available resources to the project.

Align the Organizational Personality to the Project

Understanding the biases of an organization involves three separate emphases points of view:

1. People-focused

2. Process-focused

3. Technology-focused

Mistakes can be made in the early phases of a project by introducing new technologies to a primarily process-driven organization. Conversely, BSC champions who talk about people issues to a primarily technology-focused organization may not work. Simply, understanding your organization's bias and viewpoint will guide you into introducing the ideas and technology of BSC. More often than not, BSC champions are focused on introducing the concept of BSC to their peers and management. Many can do better to understand the way and through which lens these peers and management view their worlds. Let's explore some stereotypical perspectives for all three views.

People-focused organizations tend to:

- View their world through human issues
- Believe that if people are motivated and happy, all is well
- Believe that profits are important but people must be content for profits to be achieved
- Believe that layoffs are traumatic and not an option
- Believe that firings are contemplated for a long time
- Train and develop their people

- Permit Human Resources and Management to guide the company
- Believe that communication is key

Process-focused organizations tend to

- Get really excited about organized initiatives
- Get things done by project management
- Use TQM, Process centric
- View the world through finite processes, activities, and tasks
- Value you if you are a member of a process
- Tend to have operating teams rule
- Let product lifecycles drive products rather than products driving lifecycles

Technology-driven organizations tend to

- Be bits-and-bytes oriented
- Be the first to upgrade systems
- Be IT-focused and motivated
- Enjoy the latest and greatest technological development
- Adopt new technology early
- Be very change driven and sometimes forget about evolutionary change and compatibilities

Naturally, organizations can display any one of these tendencies at different times, and they can also display various tendencies within large organizations. Every organization has an underlying harmonic of a personality that is probably not hard to one or the other but somewhere in between. Exhibit 6.4 can assist in understanding the organizational center of gravity.

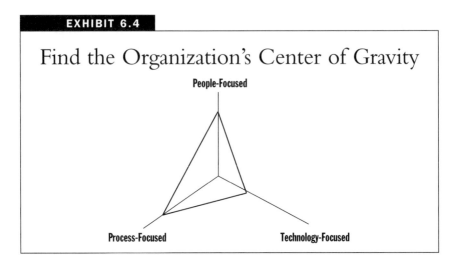

EXHIBIT 6.4

Find the Organization's Center of Gravity

People-Focused

Process-Focused   Technology-Focused

Let's assume that you have drawn these biases to that shown in the exhibit. Essentially, your organization deals with issues with the following priority:

1. Technology

2. People

3. Process

Taking a strong look at your BSC objectives, and the ways in which to approach (or have approached) a project, outline the personality and *center of gravity* of the BSC program. The center of gravity is the unique balance of these three priorities within the organization. If the BSC project is not aligned, then the project is creating a paradox in introducing the goals and objectives with the natural biases of the audience. Exhibit 6.5 shows such a paradox. Steve Sharp, chairman of the board of TriQuint Semiconductor, is a good example of an enlightened CEO who recognized the center of gravity of his organization. His story is discussed in this chapter's "In the Real World."

Exhibit 6.6 illustrates eight bias maps for your project introduction and planning. When you introduce ideas and new methods to your organization, match their biases so as to find anchors for your project.

EXHIBIT 6.5

Find the Organization's Paradox

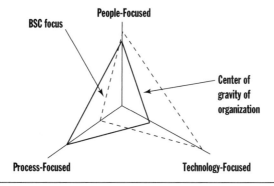

People-Focused

BSC focus

Center of gravity of organization

Process-Focused   Technology-Focused

EXHIBIT 6.6

BSC Bias Mapping Chart

People	Process	Technology	Possible Condition
High	High	High	The project may lack focus. High achieving in nature
High	High	Low	Focus on people and process issues. Structured methods are important. Technology partners may be selected later. Technology training is necessary. Management may consider having consultants to select technology.
High	Low	High	People and technology focused Beware that human issues divert objectives. Fad technologies may divert project. Consider bringing in consultant/ project manager.
High	Low	Low	People-centric Insensitive to cause-and-effect relationships

EXHIBIT 6.6 CONTINUED

People	Process	Technology	Possible Condition
			Politics of people may kill project orientation. Priority may be to maintaining relationships.
Low	Low	Low	Nowhere's land. Don't attempt anything.
Low	High	High	Process and technology focused People/communication lacking emphasis Consider consultant to contain project. Create communications systems. Remove fear.
Low	Low	High	Technology is worshipped. "Ready-fire-aim"" mentality Belief system—technology over-comes all. Consider process consultation. Consider communications consultant.
Low	High	Low	Process-centric Acceptance criteria: Fits into process Technology training is necessary. Communication process may work.

Educate the Enterprise

Those who have a plan to educate their teams and organizations tend to create and re-enforce the need for BSC-based information. BSC champions learn about BSC through books, conferences, and user groups, among other ways. Their learning is usually rapid while the learning of their organization is much slower. BSC project success can be co-related with the level of learning and commitment of the organization as a whole. For BSC to fully deploy knowledge to the desktop of operating teams and for them to make good decisions with this information, teams all around the organization must learn about BSC and its value to decision making.

Chapter 7 discusses the technology adoption cycle in BSC as education, pilot, and enterprise. Projects move from one phase to the next, in sequence (see Exhibit 6.7). Individuals, teams, and organizations also take the similar learning path. In a BSC project, several forces resist this learning:

- The inertia of the way things are
- The inertia of fearing the unknown; what is known is safer
- The inertia of learning without tools and focus
- The inertia of too much to do
- The inertia of being measured on other performance measures
- The inertia of fearing loss of job security

Exhibit 6.7 illustrates the challenges and information demands that might require focused education in climbing this BSC power curve.

The seminal work of Peter Senge in the *Fifth Discipline* has focused us onto the art and science of collective organizational learning. BSC

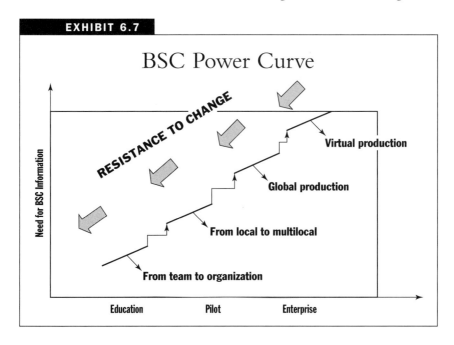

EXHIBIT 6.7

BSC Power Curve

programs start, grow, and die with "learning disabilities"[4] as their poison. Does your organization have any learning techniques that have worked in the past? How does your organization learn new ideas and implement them? Does your organization have blind spots; that is, do they not notice people issues? Exhibit 6.8 illustrates a sample, organized approach to identifying the learning tools in a BSC project.

Understanding Self Demands Careful Observation

Steven Covey[5], one of the more popular thought leaders and authors of our time, has often been quoted as asking us to seek to understand before being understood.

Ultimately, the failure of the BSC educational process is seldom a failure of the team or organization. It is usually a failure of mismatching the educational tools and techniques with the methods of learning and communicating within an organization. One can force this learning by getting the person in the corner office to dictate the need and the methods of technology and methodology absorption. One can get very far with this, in fact, but all that results is a short-term high-amplitude event. CEOs will seldom have the bandwidth to keep the attention and the loud voice on this topic indefinitely. BSC, if introduced effectively, might never stay the same; it might mutate to serve the way business is done rather than remain an initiative. Before you embark on your journey, ask some of the questions listed to gain a true understanding of the characteristics of your audience. The questions themselves will wake up your audience and prepare them for your next actions:

- What have you heard about BSC in our organization?
- What are the objectives of this initiative?
  - To downsize?
  - To improve processes?
  - To discover our true implementation guidelines?
  - To understand how strategy turns to action?

EXHIBIT 6.8

Resistance Busters: Tools for Educating the Enterprise

	Operations		BSC Team		Corporation		CEO	
	Priority	Phase	Priority	Phase	Priority	Phase	Priority	Phase
Presentations								
BSC conferences			9	e				
User group invites	1	p	2	p				
Videos			5	e,p				
Distance learning	2		7	p,pr				
On-site demos			6	e,p				
On-site rapid prototyping	3	e	3	e			7	
On-site seminars			4	e				
Public seminars	5	p						
Speakers							2	
Thought leader visits			1	e			1	
Newsletters from vendors	4	p						
Books	6	e						
White papers							3	
Success stories	7	p	8	pr			4	
Magazine articles								
E-mail messages							5	
Fax machine messages								
Templates of reports								
Web site/intranet info	8	pr					6	

Phases are:
e = education; p = pilot; pr = production

105

- Who sponsored the initiative?
- Are our competitors using it?
- What is it?
- What are the key business issues we are seeking help to solve?
- Do you think this is a Trojan horse for downsizing exercise?
- Have we succeeded in our previous initiatives? Why or why not?
- Do you believe this is another initiative, or a new way of doing business?
- How much time do we need to be trained?
- Have you read or seen anything on BSC?
- What technologies do you use, and how often do you use them?
- How much time do you have to analyze data?
- What percentage of input do you get from the following?
  - E-mail
  - Voice-mail
  - Internet
  - In-basket
  - Meetings
  - Seminars
  - Faxes
  - Phone calls
  - Forums
- What do you automatically remove from your desk?
- What is the biggest challenge BSC will face?
- How many people are involved with BSC?
- What is the standard database system you use?
- Which is the data warehouse you use?
- How do you budget?
- Which ERP (enterprise resource planning) system is being implemented and used?

- Does your IT group employ a best-of-breed tools strategy, or do you have to follow the specified systems provided?
- How often do people survey you?
- Do you believe we should hire outside consultants?
- Are you part of a team and does it follow a process?
- What is the optimal team size and composition?

BSC projects that spend the time to analyze the behavior of the clients of the information can articulate reports that work. Else, reports fall on desks of decision makers and never change behaviors because they are not reflecting the interests and focus of these leaders.

Information Can Behave Differently

Information behavior, when loosely defined, means how people approach and handle information. It introduces a very relevant tool to understanding the educational inabilities of your organization. Information behavior can be applied to how users use BSC information. Prior to developing a plan to educate the various constituents of your organization, information behavior must be understood as it affects how we can plan, develop, and implement technologies.[6]

There are two ways to view how information is handled:

1. *Shadowing.* Observation is far more powerful a research tool than questionnaires. Watch the clients of your educational program and see what they read, watch, and learn.

2. *Know the users' technology preferences.* Watch what media they use to do their work. Do they read e-mail, intranet information bases, or use paper?

Using these observations, try to map their specific preferences to the media available to you to educate and inform them.

How to Approach Educating Your Organization

First, we should identify who our audiences are. In each phase, our audience increases to include new entrants, for example, IT professionals, manufacturing personnel, and so on. Two strategies can be used to educate: *rifleshot approach* and *buckshot approach*.

In the rifleshot approach:

- Educate only on a need to know basis.
- The project takes a skunk-works form so that you can gain traction and prove your concept before others destroy the opportunity.
- Resistance may not come prematurely.
- Once you get proof of your concept, top management might not buy into it.

In the buckshot approach:

- You are going for maximum leverage and breadth.
- Educate the CEO and executive management and gain consensus.
- Educate as a major program in the company.
- Address all resistance up front while developing a proof of concept.
- Resistance will come in the form of debate.
- It may never begin and remain stagnant in debate.

Moving from Agreement to Commitment

Often, teams agree that they will achieve a goal and try to do it to the best of their ability. Effort is seldom worth a passing grade when it comes to BSC projects. The well-respected Apollo 13 mission gained the attention of the world when its story was put on the big screen. The mission captured the hearts of Americans because it was filled with heroic deeds in the face of disaster. The best part was that they made it back alive against all odds. The drama and courage displayed in this event over-shadowed the fact that they failed in their mission to land on the moon.

BSC projects run similarly—if you don't get to the goal line, playing the game can be celebrated with balloons and wall plaques for the project that almost made it. At the end of the day, there is no replacement for the commitment to completing your project and with the necessary information to make the right decisions. The BSC project team and the management of the endeavor must be moved from agreement to commitment for project success by first knowing the difference between the two:

Agreement is:

- I will try to make it work.
- It's good, we'll try it.
- I hope everyone sacrifices.
- If it fails, I know I would have learned a lot.

Commitment is:

- I will make it work.
- It's a sacrifice but the returns are clear.
- It will not fail because the corporation will not fail.

The primary method to gain commitment for BSC is to get upper management buy-in to resource commitments up front.

Top management will only buy in to BSC if it recognizes the true value that it can provide in realigning the operations of the organization, but many times it combines with external forces that cause notable acceptance to the cause. One major pull for commitment is the change in market dynamics—for example, consolidation in the banking market or loss of revenues and market-share in the semiconductor business, and so on. In these situations, BSC may end up on the CEO's radar screen. If this is not the case, five common buy-in methods exist:

1. *Taste testing.* In this method, using short and small pilots in an attempt to prove the concept and the opportunity may work.

2. *Mikey likes it!* This technique involves using industry benchmarks to drive BSC as the method of choice. Within your industry, you may prove that a wave of BSC initiatives have produced results. Using the outside influence and need to drive internal acceptance will hasten commitment.

3. *Doctor says so!* This technique involves using outside consultants and educators to convince management of the knowledge leadership your organization can attain. You can use books, videos, and other collaterals to convince management that these techniques have proven competent.

4. *Trust your wingman.* This technique involves using the informal leaders within your organization to influence management. Since they are trusted confidants, they may play the role of the trusted bishop whispering in the queen's ear.

5. *Ride the wave.* In any organization, many initiatives take the attention of management. Here you would convince management that BSC feeds or drives these key initiatives. In numerous organizations, BSC has fed and focused the performance measurement programs called *key performance indicators (KPIs)*. KPIs are designed to establish and measure performance goals within teams. Teams are measured periodically on achieving the performance goals and are rewarded based on their achievement. Introducing BSC without any linkage to KPIs would be a recipe for being ignored. Many times, there is tremendous linkage between these goals and BSC. Understanding an organizational footprint is the first step to designing a complete and successful BSC program.

IN THE REAL WORLD

Triquint Dials into Change Management

Steve Sharp, long-time CEO of TriQuint Semiconductor and current chairman of the board, a leading supplier of high-performance components and modules for communications applications, took the helm in 1991. At approximately $24 million in revenue, the company was looking for leadership in getting it to the next level. Steve's mission and the mission of the company was to get to profitability quickly. Then he asked the second question—what do we want to be?

Sharp was an outsider. He wanted to set the right tone for what was ahead. He also wanted to develop a set of shared values to run the company. He brought the team together in an offsite to prepare them for the upcoming task of a possible layoff. He decided that the best way to understand them as leaders and for them to know his style and beliefs was to formulate their value statements together. Sharp credits the company's ability to challenge itself based on the value statements they generated.

Through this exercise, TriQuint's value statements were established, which has taken the organization through to the multimillion-dollar revenue generator that it is.

Summary

- How do you identify your organizational readiness for change?

- How do you identify if your change leaders personality fits the task at hand?

- What is transformation–relevant leadership?

111

- What is task-relevant leadership?
- What is task-relevant readiness?
- What are the three personalities of a change-ready organization?

Success Factor Two: Understand the Balanced Scorecard Learning Cycle

After reading this chapter, you will be able to

- Recognize the four stages of development of BSC in the organization.
- Understand the characteristics of the education, pilot, and enterprise phase of development.
- Recognize how technology enables the five phases of BSC growth in the organization.
- Differentiate between a fad and long-term transformation.

In observing Balanced Scorecard (BSC) implementations worldwide, certain common characteristics emerge. Many BSC endeavors grow through certain growth and learning phases prior to implementation. Some endeavors, however, fail to reach their true potential—that is, they never go beyond piloting. Why?

There are many reasons why but one of the main reasons is that companies take on too much too fast in their project and do not respect the basic elements that are needed to build and sustain an endeavor. Successful companies view BSC as a way of life rather than an endeavor. If one considers implementation as the establishing of a new way of life, one would be more patient, methodical, and use more of a building-block approach.

If organizations do not consider BSC a new way of living, BSC will be another fad.

Comparatives of Fads versus Long-Term Transformation

BSC has been able to overcome the label of being a fad. Today, a large portion of the Fortune 100 is working with or is in the process of implementing BSC. It has overcome some of the basic challenges with fad management techniques:

- Limited life
- Desires to indoctrinate organization rather than transform
- Use consultants and do not transfer knowledge
- One book away from being stopped
- Usually unintegrated information
- Part-time teams
- Visionary leaders
- Quick-fix oriented
- Immediate value search
- Standalone
- Inexpensive
- Proprietary
- Closed architecture
- Limited service, support, and training
- Limited upgrades and updates to creation
- Frequent *Ahas!*

Business transformation, however, really gets deeper into the fabric of an organization and has the following characteristics:

- A way of doing business
- A regiment

- Competitive advantage
- Dedicated teams
- Integrated
- Pragmatic leader
- A living "diet plan"
- Long-term value with immediate side effects
- Scalable and maintainable
- Higher price/performance
- Standards based
- Open architecture
- Strong service, support, and training
- Applications services component
- Regular upgrades and updates
- Frequent "I knew that" as confirmation

Fads tend to be unidimensional and have the promise of a quick fix. BSC hardly fits this billing. Some organizations do design their BSC endeavors as a quick fix and a one-shot event. Naturally, they get what they set out to build.

The valued difference to other initiatives is found in the following areas:

- BSC is about managing and balancing the business using multiple dimensions, that is, perspectives, and serves the great need of cascading strategy into action throughout the organization.
- Technology exists to transform the viewing of the organization from this new perspective.
- Several organizations have already worked with and institutionalized BSC for several years and a large body of knowledge and experience now exists.

Technology tends to prolong knowledge and organizational memory. When systems exist to retain, transform data into information, and deliver it to the desktop, the probability of transforming what may begin as a fad into a way of doing business is greater. The reinforcement delivered by technology that is truly integrated and continuous is significant.

Cycle Phases of a BSC Project

Four distinct phases of the cycle of a BSC project have emerged through the years (see Exhibit 7.1):

1. Trigger phase

2. Education phase

3. Pilot phase

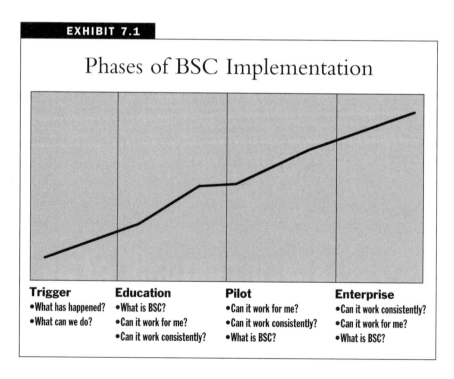

EXHIBIT 7.1

Phases of BSC Implementation

Trigger	Education	Pilot	Enterprise
•What has happened?	•What is BSC?	•Can it work for me?	•Can it work consistently?
•What can we do?	•Can it work for me?	•Can it work consistently?	•Can it work for me?
	•Can it work consistently?	•What is BSC?	•What is BSC?

4. Enterprise phase

- Local enterprise phase
- Global enterprise phase
- Virtual enterprise phase

Let's take a look at each of these phases in detail.

Trigger Phase

Most BSC programs are launched to solve a set of problems. Very seldom is BSC employed as a natural course of doing business, that is, just to improve it. "Business units fail to re-focus because they are pre-occupied with the present or the past. "Success is a double-edged sword,"[1] states John Whitney, Professor of Management at Columbia University's School of Business in New York City, when discussing how success in the past or present can "lull a company into complacency." As BSC is more understood, more organizations will adopt this method as a natural course of business. Today, it takes a "pain" of some sort to motivate organizations to adopt BSC. A trigger of some sort, be it competitive pressures, a need for better and more accurate deployment of strategy, a loss in momentum, or an actual loss in revenues or profit, are common examples of triggers. In the public sector, legislative or mission-driven mandates can create triggers. In the case of the Naval Undersea Warfare Center in Newport Rhode Island, the trigger was fueled by the need to create a customer-driven organization[2] but triggered by the Government Performance and Results Act (GPRA) of 1993. Further triggers for them were the Government Management Reform Act of 1994 and the Information Technology Management Reforms Act of 1996.

In these cases, the shock of loss or failure usually widens peoples' pupils and they tend to search for alternatives to improvement. Characteristically, most companies in this situation look for the quick fix and resort to BSC for support.

Examples of triggers are:

Industry	Market and Internal Triggers
Medical/Healthcare	Customer-directed healthcare/cost of delivering services
Utilities	Global privatization
Government	Having more to do with less budget
	Budget justification and impact statements
	Outsourcing
Banking/Finance	Consolidation and acquisition
	Optimization of delivery and differentiation
Groceries/Food	Optimization of operating capacity in a highly competitive space where margins are challenged

All in all, external forces create the need for considering new methods of management. In the end, certain conditions foster the invitation of BSC as the primary activity.

One cautionary word—it is usually at this phase that BSC is viewed as the answer to all ills. Teams and champions tend to promise more than they can deliver and set the conditions for failure. BSC is not designed to solve all ills; it is focused on key deliverables as mentioned in prior chapters.

However, organizations do not jump into the BSC wave because they like more things to do; they are usually attempting to solve a problem(s) that they cannot ignore. At this point, they seek to learn new ways and encounter the BSC methodology.

Education Phase

Born from the desks of finance and accounting yet focused on strategy implementation, most BSC aficionados believe that BSC endeavors are only getting more and more mainstream. This is all true—BSC *is* becoming more mainstream as more and more companies are adopting the philosophy. However, there is a much larger group of people to be educated on BSC than those who understand it and practice it.

Even though BSC is well known, what and how to implement it is not yet mainstream. Consequently, when corporate-champions get involved with BSC they tend to absorb information very fast and sometimes forget that they must educate the vast array of people back in the office. Frustrated with the lack of acceptance from their organizations, the champions of BSC often think that their colleagues are behind the times. This is not true. They are merely displaying the classic learning curve challenges found in many organizations. If left alone to the natural progress, the organization will make learning difficult rather than simple and organized. The organization is facing and entering the educational phase of the learning. This is one of the most important phases in the learning life cycle. If performed well, this learning can translate into countless saved years of ineffectiveness.

This educational phase brings the foundation necessary for the organization to accept, employ, and deploy BSC. At this phase, champions and their teams are asking only one question before all others: "What is it?" Other questions like, "Will it work for me?" or, "Will it work continuously?" take second and third to the main question.

Watching several BSC implementations, one could come to the conclusion that the implementation curve from pilot to propagation is directly proportional to the learning curve within the organization in question. If an organization teaches the value of BSC and the organization really learns, the adoption and deployment curve of BSC will be accelerated.

Often underestimated, the education phase of a project is usually done quickly and locally to the project team. Cascadia Partners LLC, an Oregon-based venture capital firm, did not do that. It started with trying to build a strategy map that gave people the motivation necessary to pursue performance measurement and BSC (see "In The Real World" in this chapter). Formal educational programs are a necessary and sufficient condition for project ignition and success. Yet, consistent and continuous training and feedback are essential to effectiveness. Saturn Corporation's CEO, Richard G. LeFauvre, states, "If you think education is expensive, just try ignorance."[3]

This phase is one that never ends in a BSC program. The audience of learners will grow if the project scope grows. Education can take several forms:

- Formal education found in seminars, training courses, and academic institutions
- Informal learning found in *Webinars*, Web-based learning, on-the-job training, mentoring, and consultants

All in all, this phase is the most important and should be planned carefully because every other phase depends on this being executed well.

Education is the key to learning but the reasons behind why organizations will learn are more complex. The trigger phase gets individuals to pick up the idea and then get educated. The education phase is where individuals ask questions and find answers to the pressing need. When they find BSC, they will now want to put it to the test—or pilot.

Pilot Phase

Pilot phase is the trial phase. Once in pilot programs, BSC champions and teams are trying to prove the concept of BSC and also pilot test the ability of the organization to accept the methodology. In the middle of the evolution curve, multifunction teams usually form. These teams focus on the following:

- Self-training and education
- Development of basic models
- Using stand-alone modeling environments usually PC-based

- Being guided by external consultants or educators
- Searching for the *Ahas!* to impress the management with the value of the team
- Selling management and the operating teams on the value of the program

These teams are trying to answer the basic question of "Will it work?" above any other. Note that some pilots almost look like enterprise rollouts because they have global deployment implementations; they have multimodeling teams across many regions and seem to use the information at the operational level. They are still pilots because they are not the mainstream business method. Pilots have certain characteristics:

- Tend to be short and make a point
- Four to five perspectives chosen and experimented with
- Encouraged by management rather than expected by management
- Behave like other initiatives with a lot of dust in the sky and loud fanfares
- Live fast and die, with no one person fully dedicated to them
- Have a 50–50 chance of survival
- Half-life is two years
- Defined measures

Most important, one must ensure that if all goes well, someone does something and makes decisions with the information. The most frustrating challenge to a champion is to accept that a great project ended in no decisions and changes. Anticipating this, the best way to teach your organization to respond is to give it mock-up reports of information and test its reactions by asking, "If I got you this, what decisions would you make?"

When driving a pilot project, performance measures are chosen and defined. Usually, this is done with an eye to the fact that these measures will be modified once the project is launched. This informality can destroy the simplicity of the project and turn it into a complex search for measures found in several parts of the organization. The Naval Undersea Warfare Center at Newport, Rhode Island, team found that after one year of work, the number of measures were increasing and added in an "add-hoc" manner.

As their leadership changed, new measures were added. There was need for a "mechanism to discern whether a new measure should or should not be added and consequently the number of measures continued to grow."[a] One mechanism is a performance measure dictionary, which will:

- Identify all performance measures
- Define the purpose of the measures
- Establish what the sample measures are
- Direct the location of these measures
- Explain the basis that this measure exists
- Define the output and outcome measure for the measure
- Define an owner for the measure
- Define the objective and perspective that drive this measure

This performance measure dictionary can be online and should have a set of criteria and conditions for addition. It should also be managed and maintained by one individual or team.

On a cautionary word, when part of a pilot project, make sure to test not just the system concept but the following:

- Acceptance of the concept
- Ability of the organization to understand and engage on the topic

James Collins and Jerry Porras, authors of *Built to Last: Successful Habits of Visionary Companies*[4] state:

> Having a great idea or being a charismatic visionary leader is "time telling"; building a company that can prosper far beyond the presence of any single leader and through multiple product life cycles is "clock building."

In the same way, pilot programs are time-telling exercises; a proof of concept and test of the possibilities. Production system implementation is the proof of clock building and the test of the realities created through the dreams and visions of pilot programs. When the team is ready to start a pilot, ask the following questions as a guide to know where in the organization the pilot should begin:

- Where would the project be most visible, that is, a burning platform looking for a solution?
- Is the area in consideration bounded with all the necessary information and people and scope?
- Is there a business owner in the operational side of the business and a champion ready to serve?

- If the project were to be done here, is the team going to be too large to be effective?

- What about the data and performance measurement demands, both in terms of data quality and in terms of accessibility?

Enterprise Phase

The enterprise phase is a natural consequence to the successful pilot. However, as much as 50 percent of pilots never go to another phase—they either die or remain in a limbo of satisfaction. One reason why (there are many reasons) is that many companies do not anticipate the technical requirements of this phase when doing a pilot.

In a pilot, we architect our systems for the quick hit. The meantime between initiation and results is short, and the requirements for accuracy, repeatability, and maintainability are low. Many times, BSC project leaders cut corners to achieve the "big bang" they are seeking. After the applause dies down and the plaques for victory are distributed and hung, someone on the team is usually asked to make this work all the time with the same temporary resources. The second time is less exciting and the champion is unable to cut corners and build short-term solutions like before.

The demands of enterprise deployment include:

- Regular data integration demands

- Regular data-gathering methods for all the necessary information

- Regular ways of getting empirical information, that is, information found in people's heads

- Custom reports developed and adjusted to the needs of operational teams and managers

- Constant education to all concerned on BSC

- Regular orientation to new participants

- Competency centers to assist any user of computing systems

- IT is involved and sees the need for standards to protect the investment

- Automation becomes a significant goal because manual translation of information is challenging

Production systems like these or on-line systems can be varied in nature for BSC. That is, when champions talk of their implementations, a careful examination is necessary because the same words sometimes mean different situations. Enterprise could mean:

- I have built a pilot model of a small business unit and am now going to expand that model to a larger enterprise.

- I have completed my basic model for a site and now I shall build other site models.

- The business unit is now using BSC language but has yet to automate the activities.

- I want to model my entire enterprise (i.e., models developed across my multinational company).

- I want to deploy scorecards across my enterprise moving data that are financially endorsed, IT-maintained, and operationally used by decision makers using desktop tools.

Clearly, some of these enterprise deployments are local (within a certain country or region) while others are global (among countries and nations), and they need the involvement of different teams in implementation. Such a system requires significant enterprise deployment control systems. The true global deployment demands significant resource commitment and checks-and-balances or else you will repeat the same mistake across the globe. For example, you must ensure that you have some design controls on the models you create across the globe. Each site, if left to itself, will create its own model in its own way. When a consolidated view of the models is wanted, trouble begins. However, if control is everything in the structure and the data of the models, the various anomalies to change in improving your company-architecture will never surface.

Here are seven suggestions:

1. Force a standard dictionary for your performance metrics and objectives, that is, outlining a common language for model usage.

2. To allow for cultural differences across regions, allow for certain variations in the model and scorecard design and ensure that a sign-off or certification occurs.

3. Develop manuals for model design, scorecard creation, and reporting specific to your business.

4. Train a competency center to support the systems you are creating and to be a clearinghouse for consistency.

5. Have a champion travel to each site to ensure problems are removed or solved. Sometimes, this champion travels to each plant and ensures that models are developed consistently. This is one way to get the job of consistency done fast, but beware that only this person knows how and what has been created. A back-up champion should be put into a plan just in case.

6. Test all technologies to consolidate models, link other business transformation information and systems, that is, ABC/M or Six Sigma information and ensure consistency across the enterprise before going into implementation.

7. Ensure that all sites report regularly, that is, once a quarter, and ensure that the scorecard can be refreshed once a quarter at least using the most up-to-date processes.

Virtual Enterprise

New technologies are being introduced daily, thanks to companies like Microsoft Corporation that are making the networks of tomorrow almost transparent. With the advent of intranets and extranets, information will be delivered to users and accessible without any knowledge on the part of where the information is based. Users will be talking to a server in Japan and may not need to know.

Consequently, the future BSC environment will be almost virtual, where knowledge on the desktop will appear via a simple browser accessing scorecard information from several consolidated models across the universe of models in the company. Some BSC environments are based off *push technologies*, that is, you have to push information out to the desktop and to managers, and so on. These managers then review the information and interrogate the data. Other information technologies will be *pull technologies*. The manager will be able to set personality-requests on her system and allow the system to collect information under the conditions specified by her. Disregarding all other information, certain BSC conditions will be recorded and informed to the manager. The systems will understand users and their personal needs.

This virtual enterprise phase is around the horizon and within grasp of the leading technology companies. However, technology deployment does not create enterprise deployment, people make it happen and business processes within organizations enable consistency and continuity within these organization. No technology change can establish processes within companies. The source of all change is found in the assets that leave for home every day.

Questions to Ask

1. How are you going to ensure that learning about BSC is constant, consistent, and continuous?

2. What operational methods are planned to ensure an effective pilot program? Do you have a set of criteria that records and measures success at the pilot phase?

3. What is your definition of when you are ready to achieve enterprise deployment? Are the things you are doing in the pilot program going to hinder or enable the enterprise deployment?

IN THE REAL WORLD

Venture Capital Firm Maps Its Future

Cascadia Partners LLC was a seventeen-year-old early-stage private equity firm simultaneously evaluating its core strategy and reconstituting the partnership. Strategy mapping can be a very simple way of visualizing strategy within its chosen perspectives. Consider Exhibit 7.2, a strategy map for Cascadia Partners. After raising and investing four prior funds that were each $25 million or less, the firm decided to build a new fund of approximately $100 million. With experienced talent within new market dynamics, it is forming a new strategy. Cascadia Partners realized that it had two key strategic themes:

❶ Raise $100 million in investment funds.

❷ Achieve a sufficiently strong Internal Rate of Return so that it could win the next investment from its Limited Partners.

Cascadia Partners is now on the second phase of its scorecard evolution. It is evaluating performance measures for each strategic initiative and is evaluating the in-depth cause-and-effect relationships. It discusses the strategy map elements weekly, sometimes changing the interdependencies but always acting on the new discoveries using the framework as guide.

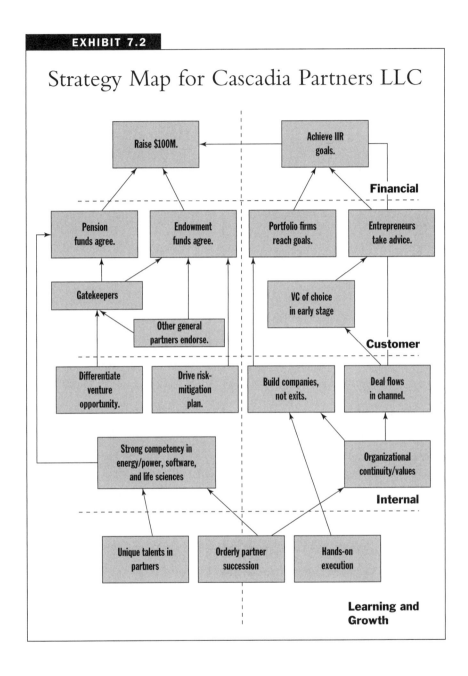

EXHIBIT 7.2

Strategy Map for Cascadia Partners LLC

Summary

Differentiate between a fad and long-term transformation. Fads are always sold as long-term transformations but certain characteristics were defined in this chapter to help the reader get clear on the difference. BSC is not a fad but a transformational solution to the problem of alignment. But one cannot implement this methodology just by jumping into it without respecting the phases of understanding and growth with BSC.

The four stages any analytic application goes through in an organization are:

1. *Trigger phase.* At this phase something drives the need for change and reevaluation.

2. *Education phase.* At this phase, the champion and team start to look at what methods and technology and people can get them from where they are to their targets. They ask the question, "What works?"

3. *Pilot phase.* At this phase, the organization is able to test this new method, technology, and people on a small, bounded project.

4. *Enterprise phase.* With the success of a pilot, the organization drives for a full enterprisewide project ensuring that everyone is involved and is making it a part of his or her everyday activities.

Each of these phases is critical to the adoption of both methodology and technology in an organization. Missing any one of the steps usually results in the organization retracing to the steps prior. Some BSC implementation jumps into the last phase and has to go back to education and pilot phases.

CHAPTER 8

Success Factor Three: Know the Road Map for Implemention

After reading this chapter, you will be able to

- Recognize characteristics of a doomed BSC exercise.
- Implement a BSC project.
- Create a road map for activities around a BSC system.

Businesses have found that BSC uncovers tremendous opportunity for optimization between strategy and action.

In previous chapters, we have focused on the understanding necessary for successful implementations. Without understanding the true potentiality and strategic position a BSC system provides, many programs have fallen short of expectations.

One major factor that enables BSC continuity is deploying technology that is manageable, scaleable, and repeatable. The other factor involves the process and people components—that is, a strong project orientation to the program. A key learning aspect for these companies is that, early on, they decided that a phased approach to implementation was best. A phased approach is invaluable because of the dynamics of many BSC endeavors. First, many BSC teams are populated with multifunction members who have other primary functions. Some BSC projects can last years, and a phased approach with measured deliverables creates signposts for success, as well as allows team members to know when to move to the next phase, sometimes with different people. It also permits them to spend less time on the rules of engagement and more time on generating results because all the rules that run the project are defined.

BSC's Other Three Technology Perspectives

There are as many ways to manage a BSC program as there are personalities in one. Although most programs hunt for the ultimate *Aha!* with data gathered over a pilot program, those that succeed have other common traits. One strong trait of successful BSC programs is project management and scheduling. Just like all other endeavors, a carefully planned project has a greater chance for success, and also a greater chance to be flexible and to bring along the team that takes it on.

Good technology project management can transform objectives into software-based models and then to reports that can assist users to make better management decisions. To ensure that, the end result of a technology project management process is the creation of a program that is scaleable, manageable, and repeatable:

- *Scaleable.* The ability to grow the architecture of the endeavor and to bring larger and larger amounts of data, build ever growing models of the enterprise, and to report to an expanded amount of people.

- *Manageable.* The ability to contain the physical work and to contain the cost of keeping the system going.

- *Repeatable.* The ability to replicate this in multiple locations using the same techniques and the same technologies.

Characteristics of a Doomed BSC Exercise

The following story outlines distinct phases to a doomed BSC exercise. First, management, in conjunction with the program sponsor, hands down the objectives, and the project is staffed. The team immediately swarms the organization teams with questions and questionnaires, and these questions face resistance within the organization. Thus, educational meetings are set up to explain the questions and overcome fear of change.

Now the project will begin generating excitement. People will buy in to the idea that this project promises to cure the common cold, and management will receive notes encouraging that the change begin. The project team will start gathering data. Employees will be interviewed to determine what they do and how they help others. Now there will be silence, as the project team begins the data integration phase in which they and the IT professionals collect other data for their models. They find that 70 percent of the information is found in people's heads and have to now go for interviews or a new survey tool.

Now the model is ready to be built, and management sees progress while they are fielding cautious questions from the operating teams, who say that they are not sure about the information. There are multiple sources of performance information and the data are "dirty,"—that is, they are not consistent and need to be cleaned up. Months have gone by and the project team is hard at work building the models and scorecards. Finally, they are ready for the presentation. They are only a month late with the information.

The presentation to management is a roaring success. The managers give the team a standing ovation and multiple plaques to hang on their cubicle walls. As the clapping dies down, however, the managers now wish to make adjustments to the models and the scorecards. More questions have come out of the exercise than before. The team dare not tell them that they put these models and scorecards together fast and that some of the questions might require them to redesign the models and gather more data. Furthermore, three members of the team must return to their real jobs.

Management has seen the opportunities and is now blind with enthusiasm. They send the team to their next project with bigger expectations with the same resources. Now the team approaches the same data sources and interviews with the same vigor. Meanwhile, the operating teams have heard nothing except that the meeting was a success. They are weary of further questions and answers. They offer no new information because there are no rewards.

The project team presents to them. In horror, the operating teams exclaim that the data they obtained were only estimates and that the results must be wrong. In fact, things have changed in the last six months. They challenge the entire process—and the methodology, as well. Furthermore, they now realize that they will be using PC-based systems to interrogate this model and obtain answers to the most pressing of questions. They are hardly trained on a scorecarding system like this and now realize that they need more resources.

The IT group hears of this project in a meeting and now declares that they must certify the technology and ensure that no corruption of information in their data stores has occurred. Not only that, but they believe that the technology used is inferior and to support this, they must get funded. Meanwhile, management is waiting for answers to new questions and is beginning to believe that the BSC team leader lacks the skills to continue the project because of all the complaints they are hearing about. They ask, "Maybe this stuff called BSC isn't real?"

The project team now states the challenges:

- A resistant team
- A nonscaleable and nonmanageable model-set with scorecards
- An unintegrated application environment
- A lack of funding and resources
- A plan to re-vamp the system and produce results that will take double the time for the pilot

The program is delayed until further notice.

The abovementioned scenario is a typical example of a mismatch of expectations and resources in a project. Miscommunication, unreasonable expectations are a few of the reasons why projects fail.

BSC Project Implementation Phases

Often, doomed BSC endeavors end with the loud roar at the finish line, followed by solemn silence. The following outlines the phases of a BSC project that can produce continuous effectiveness:

- Pick your team and leadership.
- Pick your target and momentum drivers.
- Sell value always
- Pick outside help: consultants and vendors.
- Pick your objectives and the criteria for success.
- Identify corporate strategy and thrusts.
- Build the strategy maps.
- Identify drivers and performance metrics of the perspectives.
- Identify the technology platform
- Systematize feedback.
- The report-out meeting and your communications strategy
- Win the right to do it all over again.

Inherent in this project guide is the following:

- Projects never end.
- Checks and balances exist in each phase to ensure proper hand-offs to the next.
- Documentation is vital in each phase and an overall project plan must be developed prior to launch.

Pick Your Team and Leadership

In any endeavor, the team and the leader will make the difference between success and failure. All change management projects demand tremendous skills from the champion and from the team that ultimately gets things done. Resistance is expected in any project, especially a strategy mapping exercise, because some groups will soon realize that their business functions might be removed if not aligned with a strategic thrust. A large part of the BSC exercise is dedicated to aligning the actions of an organization to the key strategies. Consequently, the actions that are not aligned will probably be removed or redeployed.

The champion and team will be viewed as change agents to some, but also as the team that destroys jobs. The job of a BSC executive chartered with bringing this project to results is

- To hire and fire the champion
- To enable the selection and recruitment of a leadership team
- To protect this team and champion from unjust attack
- To set, monitor, and drive for the successful achievement of milestones
- To formally set up systems to celebrate success and to learn from failures
- To amplify the pilot project into an enterprisewide implementation

Chapter 6 discussed the leadership traits most necessary for a champion. Beyond these traits are the following necessary characteristics:

- Can the champion see the vision?
- Can the champion withstand the organizational skeptics without losing focus on the key objectives to be met?
- Does the champion have a keen sense of awareness of the new reality and not be imprisoned by the present reality?

- Does the champion have the necessary education and skills to guide the project?

- How does the champion take advice, and can the champion work with outside consultants and technology vendors?

- Does the champion have planning and project skills?

- Does the champion want to prove something to the organization?

- Can the champion communicate and set up systems for communication?

- Does the champion inspire the team?

Team dynamics can kill a BSC project. Many teams are selected randomly, but the thoughtful recruitment of a team will enhance success. Apart from the soft side to team players, consider the following skills in the transformation team:

- Analytical skills—that is, model building

- Interviewing skills

- Knowledge of BSC and associated methodologies like activity-based costing

- Technology infrastructure knowledge and application for enterprisewide deployment

- Functional representation and capability (i.e., finance, marketing, sales, and engineering knowledge can only assist in developing, designing, and marketing the objectives).

Pick Your Target and Momentum Drivers

Champions who lead a BSC program must pick an objective and a business unit to drive the learning for BSC. Many would like to have the process in place but not anyplace is ready for such a culture shift. How does a champion know where to place the first pilot?

- Ask the management team where they think the best location is?

- Look for the more enthusiastic units that want change and want to be the poster children for the pilot.

- Find out where the biggest challenges exist. This is where the biggest opportunities exist also.

- Where does your BSC team believe it can execute most effectively?

- BSC is about translating and sharing strategy. If the key strategic thrusts and initiatives are built around certain divisions or x-functional groups, then locate your BSC program there.

Sell Value Always

A significant mistake made by BSC drivers is to sell the program and the ideas to upper management and to forget to keep selling the value of the results to all layers of management. Also, key leaders in an institution rely on the feedback of their operating team leaders, and although they might have endorsed the program to you, they can change their minds if other, more pressing operational activities need to take hold.

One CEO insisted that he wanted the objectives to be held at all levels. Through the introduction of the program, individuals had to drive the scorecard process by participating and reviewing all the key measures, and so on. The CEO did not push for the results to be submitted, did not drive his scorecard to the board, and was engulfed in operational details. I think this is also a failing of management because they never pushed the value and were not champions for strategy linkages to the operating teams. Selling must go on always, and systems must be put in place to drive knowledge sharing and program management and accountability.

Pick Outside Help: Consultants and Vendors

Consultants are great to work with and can be accelerators for the BSC program. They can sort through the challenges and can also focus the organization for burst-speed into the BSC methodology. But how does a team know if a consultant is necessary?

- Do you or your team have the fundamental knowledge to carry out the program?
- Does a consultant carry more credibility to the process and is this important for progress?
- Do you want knowledge to be transferred to your team, or do you want the program launched for one time only?
- Do you have a budget that accommodates consultants?
- What assistance do you need in the endeavor?
- Do you have a fixed timeframe for a consulting engagement or do you need this relationship to be ongoing? When do you know you are complete?

One of the biggest concerns about consultants is that they come into an organization and never leave. They are driven by project success, but also by the billing to the client. As long as the organization understands that the main goals are established and mutually understood, consultants can play a significant role in the BSC journey, especially since they are experienced in multiple engagements of BSC and can bring knowledge that is not found within the organization. Given that BSC is a part of the core functionality and competence of the organization, knowledge and experience must be held within the company rather than farmed out. Hence, it would be key to establish objectives of knowledge transfer and also hold the internal team to self-sufficiency.

Pick Your Objectives and the Criteria for Success

Success comes from understanding your objectives and how to get there. The best way to understand your objectives with BSC and what a win is to your team is to perform a BSC on the BSC program. Look at the program in the same framework as BSC and ask the team the following questions:

- Does the team know the strategic thrusts, and have they mapped the causes and effects of the program?
- Can the team define the four or five perspectives for the BSC program—namely:
  - What is the customer perspective? Members within the company?
  - What is the financial perspective? Budget?
  - What is the internal perspective? What should the team do to perfect the result?
  - What is the learning and growth perspective? What must the team grow and learn and be capable of to do the program, and what learning and growth systems are needed to build a BSC capability in the organization?

If a BSC team is ready to use its own philosophy as an example for its own project, it will never know what it is like to make it happen.

Identify Corporate Strategy and Themes

Without identified strategy and an understanding of the key strategic thrusts that the organization is following, a BSC exercise will be challenged with defining it as well. If your organization has these identified, the project has a head start. If not, seek this understanding from upper management. It may be found in confidential strategic plans, business plans, or in key objectives. Sometimes, annual reports can give you a perspective. It is amazing that employees forget to read their own annual reports. If challenged, the team might have to drive for clarity with the management.

Build the Strategy Maps

Assuming that you have the strategy and strategic thrusts articulated, the key now is to bring together a mapping exercise. The mapping exercise usually requires the following:

- An *x*-functional team should be handpicked and representative of the company.

- Assemble in a conference room, preferably offsite to enable no distractions.

- The process for gaining ideas can take many forms, but the key to this exercise is to get a strategy map showing all the key perspectives, the cause-and-effect dependencies, and the key measures (at least initial).

- This is an interactive set of meetings, and the key is to listen rather than talk. As the group gains confidence in its ideas, new insights should arise from the process.

- Consultants are great for this process because they are outside of the organization and seldom bring the extra bias to the meeting.

- Ensure that the meeting is given ample time for preparation because the team must be well read in strategy—both the organization and the competition. They must have been given assigned reading prior.

- The process of strategy mapping is well documented by the Balanced Scorecard Collaborative.[1]

- Mapping creates a visual representation of the strategy within perspectives. This output will legitimize and capture the commitments of those who do not understand BSC. It will show balance, cause and effect, and how strategy can be realized at other levels.

- Strive to make the process fun instead of boring, creative instead of analytic, accurate instead of precise, and simple instead of complex.

- The art of mapping is to make a complex business simple in its expression of strategy.

Identify Performance Metrics of the Perspectives

Performance measure derivation takes the same energy as strategy mapping because it requires careful analysis and selection of what stakeholders want to see. The end result of the exercise is that an operating principle of managing with measures is in place across the corporation where all the performance measures are connected at all levels of the organization with cascaded objectives.

The key performance measures for each perspective must be in place before moving forward. The suggested steps for analyzing measures are

1. Interview stakeholders as to what they believe the best measures for each perspective is.

2. Focus on measures that cross organizational silos first. Many organizations already have performance measures, yet much of the measures are not coordinated or are cascaded within the organization. Organizations that live in silos place significant value to measures within their walls but seldom co-ordinate these measures across silos. BSC, using the perspectives that tend to cross silos, can bring these measures together.

3. Assemble a meeting with key stakeholders:
   - The tendency is to invite people who are at a particular level in the organization and to be politically correct in the invitation list.

- Invite those who can contribute to the isolation and exploitation of the performance measures. Do not invite those who do not contribute.

- Ensure that a process is identified to gather their ideas of which performance measures are applicable. Many methods, ranging from Post-it® notes on white boards to brainstorming methods, are used.

- Once the first cut is developed, take these measures and test them against the stakeholders. In the process of meeting with them, present to them the decisions that can be made in evaluating the pro-forma presentation and ask them what decisions they can make in viewing the perspectives with measures. Test the relationships between the perspectives and test also the decisions that cannot be made to understand the limits of the model that has been created. Keep selling anywhere and anytime.

Identify the Technology Platform

It is common to think that technology should not override process and people issues. Project teams that fail tend to focus on technology as the main tool for change management. However, technology vendors have developed their offering from stand-alone, PC-based systems and ERP systems for some years now. These vendors have gathered a significant amount of experience in technology change management over the years and are now very capable in assisting internal BSC teams to sort through the challenges ahead. Chapter 10 will be detailing the issues surrounding technology platform issues.

However, the key understanding necessary is that technology implementations cannot work unless the process and cultural issues are dealt with beforehand. Technology can work very effectively if the process around the technology is worked with equal vigor. In other words, expecting employees to input their scorecard information because input software is available is a futile assumption. Other factors must be in place to ensure and encourage such behavior.

Systematize Feedback

When BSC teams launch a program, there is usually a buzz in the air. Sometimes, the CEO declares the management's support for the need for BSC with scripted enthusiasm. Then the team meets at regular intervals and is seen working through issues. Suddenly, the team is out gathering data from sources both human and machine. The enthusiasm for new findings excites the other members of the company. At this point, communication tends to weaken and the process slows down while the team is analyzing and formulating. Feedback to the others fades and turns into doubt. Momentum is directly proportional to feedback. Some suggestions are

- *Fill the mirror or the mirror will be filled for you.* That is, inform others who you asked to participate of the progress even if there is nothing significant to update them about. They just want to feel part of the process.

- *Create a Web site for the internal team to review documentation but also an extranet for others who want to watch the process and want to learn more.* This will eventually help you understand who is part of the next layer of members to the program. The BSC team can now uncover where the next program can be initiated and with whom as members. When the BSC team asks for input, ensure that the overall discovery in raw form is shared with the people who went out of their way to assist them. For example, a BSC team member gathered data from a general manager of a business unit. She gave the team member a series of performance measures and some data about what has been gathered before. If the BSC team member sends her the overall data gathered from all other sources possible via a pie chart so that she can understand where her opinion stood with respect to the others, data will keep on coming. If it is a black box of information gathering, data will soon end on the second or third trial. Creating a system of feedback and communications is key to any BSC program.

Report-Out Meeting and Your Communications Strategy

Managers should review a communications plan from the BSC team prior to program ignition so that they can understand how it can contribute to the momentum of the program. Furthermore, the plan should highlight all the vehicles and time that the BSC team will be gathering and communicating information to the organization. Part of this communication plan should be a scheduled report-out meeting to the sponsors of the program. This meeting should highlight the following:

- The motivation behind BSC
- Key findings upfront with background materials following
- Key observations of how the company adopts new methodologies covering the people, process, and technology issues
- Actions going forward and the resources required and the outcome that can be expected in the next report-out meeting
- Feedback from the stakeholders on what they wish to see next

Win the Right to Do It All Over Again

BSC programs never really end; they are so critical to the operational effectiveness of an organization that their relevance never fades. Hence, the fact that a pilot program is near completion only means that there is so much more work to be done to get the BSC information and scorecarding into the hands of all employees. The BSC taskforce should not believe that it is done when it completes the initial process. The taskforce must ask for more resources and ensure that the team stays together. If not, the project will fall prey to the demons of pilot programs and never move to the next phase, which is the enterprise phase.

145

Frequently, pilot programs are run by a part-time enthusiast who believes in the concept and wants to see it work, but if the program is to move to the next phase and be taken as an operational necessity, resources must be dedicated to this function and operational teams must know that it is their job to manage the BSC philosophy.

Getting Real: Getting It Right the First Time

There are seven predictable steps in any BSC project:

1. Objectives-setting phase

2. Data-gathering phase

3. Modeling and performance-measurement-design phase

4. Integrating phase

5. Reporting phase

6. Data- and measures-replenishment phase

7. Planning phase: budgeting and forecasting

Objective-Setting Phase

Before anything gets underway, set the goal line for the pilot program. Business drives everyday, and any project that does not fulfill project objectives and have deliverables will fail. But the objectives of the BSC program must be established and clearly communicated. To the surprise of many a corporation, multiple goals and objectives have hurt BSC programs. Be specific. If BSC is being established to get everyone clear on his or her own jobs and contributions, then say so. If it is to communicate upper management's strategy and nothing else, then say that. But also get down to what are the key deliverables in the program—that is, at phase one, we will have level 1 data displayed only, not all the data for level 2 managers, and so on.

Data-Gathering Phase

The first time a project is launched, everyone is curious and forgiving when data are being gathered. It's the second and third and fourth time, after the problems begin, when the participants get tired of the questions and of the data-gathering work. But there are inherent challenges even the first time. As Harris Corporation understood during a data-gathering exercise unrelated to BSC, "for the most part, there was never one expert on all the data available."[2] The type and nature of the data being gathered is diverse and can reside in various places in the organization (see Exhibit 8.1). In some ways, the very value of integrated information is the challenge in a BSC project. There are three types of data being gathered:

1. General ledger information
2. Empirical information—information found in individuals' heads, for example, percentage of time spent on a particular activity
3. Operational information—related to driver information, that is, the number of customer calls or manufacturing information about shipments

EXHIBIT 8.1

Who Is Responsible for Performance Information?

Types of Info:	Marketing	Sales	Admin	Manu-facturing	Management	Engineering	Customers
Sales measures		●		●			
Quantity	●	●		●	●	●	●
% Time spent	●	●	●	●	●	●	●
Margin info			●				
Profit info							
Marketing info	●			●	●	●	●
Resource info		●	●				
Manu measures				●			
Costs	●			●			●

There are several ways to gather data:

- Interviews
- On-line surveys/data gathering systems
- Observations
- Classroom ad hoc Q&As
- Focus groups
- Paper surveys
- Timecards

These methods have their advantages and disadvantages. When considering any of these methods, consider the amount of time required and the level of detail truly required.

Make sure that your data gathering is focused on only items that can drive your model design and not on all the performance measures found in the universe of your project. Identify a series of primary questions and issues that affect the model design for your scorecarding. If a few key business issues drives the collection of information, then all the better. All in all, the performance data-gathering phase of the project must be well planned and executed. If it is assumed to be a one-time event, it will be, and the project will never cycle to improvement. In the planning, answers to the following questions should be composed:[3]

- How can we make it easy for data to be available? Automation can play a strong role in this area.
- How can we improve the quality and accuracy of the data? Inconsistency of data across systems is the greatest impediment to speed.
- To what extent to which is history required?
- How will data be replenished?

Modeling and Performance-Management-Design Phase

The model phase is perceived to be the most important part of the phases, but the experienced BSC champion might challenge that perception. As mentioned before, the most important part of the BSC exercise is in its design.

As in any design project, 80 percent of the costs fall in the design phase. Armed with this undisputed knowledge, many BSC projects spend the least time and energy in design. Consequently, they spend more time undesigning their design. Steven Covey[4] asks us to think with the end in mind. This mantra is the mantra of the experienced modeler.

For example, "Let's build models only after we architect them based on the questions we want answered," would be the obvious path to model nirvana. Fortunately and unfortunately, the most success one can gather from a BSC pilot is to attempt another endeavor to answer the next set of questions that the pilot has generated. The designer must model and architect a nonstatic model—one that is iterative and yet scaleable. Hence, there is no perfect way to model—just steps to the ultimate architecture.

Integrating Phase

Almost 70 percent of performance information for a BSC model is not input through the user interface. Hand-keying information is not necessary because information needed resides somewhere on some system in the organization. There are two ways to import information into the model:

1. ACSII (text-based) importing of information

2. Direct importing of data elements using a query engine that grabs info in specified formats from many systems

149

Model Building Tricks

When it comes down to the project, the more knowledge users have about the task at hand, the better their chance for success. The following ideas and hints are designed to assist in model building and design:

- *Don't be guided by how the software works. Don't jump into the software and begin modeling.* Software systems are enticing tools for building a BSC scorecard, and they can speed the process. But the first thing to do is design your system around what questions need to be answered. The software cannot build your model for you; it can only enable it.

- *Build models for a purpose.* Teams must decide and communicate the limits of their model building and ensure that the clients of this information will not be able to receive all that they want in the first step. These teams can achieve this by understanding and communicating the answers to the following questions prior to modeling:

  - Is your model designed for strategic or operational decision making?

  - How deep and wide is your model going to be?

  - Does your model go to the product and service levels or are you just doing high-level activity analysis?

  - What can be done to this model you are building after it is complete?

  - What information do you need prior to building this model, and in what form?

  - Can you replicate this model in other locations in your company, and will the performance measurement dictionary work?

  - How much education do I need to put in place to get it off the ground and keep it up?

- Have I faced integration issues early so that I do not have to get back and re-create all the model inputs once again?
- What trade-off are you willing to make with respect to the competing interests between accuracy and time taken to model?
- If I am building a prototype just to see, is it repeatable?
- Have I selected the right design methods?

Once model building starts, the requirements and expectations begin to expand as excitement grows. Project management becomes even more crucial.

- *Link models to strategy.* Suffice it to say that most BSC projects may complete pilot programs but fail to last because of the lack of upper management support. The reason upper management can't see its way among the trees in the forest is because we throw terms and definitions at managers, assuming they work with us daily as much as we work with our model daily. If you can relate the BSC exercise to strategic issues that managers are struggling with, they will reflect a new-found interest and drive to your project.

- *Milestones, measurements, and management.* Within the model-building exercise, ensure that you have mini-project milestones and measurables. Then if you measure by the mile, you can only slip by a mile.

- *Build smart models, not big models.* Companies are moving rapidly from pilot proof of concept installations to enterprisewide production system. It is encouraging to note that the BSC industry has moved beyond pilots, which are discrete events, to more on-line, active analysis and reporting systems that are more continuous. This evolution has its pitfalls and one way to avoid these pitfalls is to build models correct-by-construction. In fact, as complexity mutates, it is perceivable that organizations witness a gradual degradation of effective

TIPS & TECHNIQUES CONTINUED

decision making. The true measure of a BSC project is not how much is in your model and not even the decisions you make to improve your enterprise—it is the mean time between decisions (MTBD). If you cannot turn your model around to address decisions fast and flexibly, you lose in this market.

An increasing demand on and expectations from models will drive this complexity. As the models are asked to do more, they begin to creep into incredibly accurate and complete creations that lack flexibility, maintainability, and scalability.

Importing information from heterogeneous systems is seldom the challenge. The challenge seems to be in cleansing the raw data into a consistent form, given that it resides in various systems with various personalities. Sometimes it comes down to ensuring that "BSC" not be input as "BCS" or "B-S-C" or "B-s-c" or "CSB" and so on. Although a simplistic example, inconsistencies like these can destroy the project schedule.

This phase is very important if your project is to last past the pilot phase. With integration your model can be replenished with direct connections to data sources. This does not take away the need to gather information found only in peoples' heads, that is, empirical information.

Alan Paller, director of education and research at the Datawarehouse Institute in Bethesda Maryland, said, "70 percent of the labor that goes into maintaining data repositories is spent reconciling and cleaning up data."[5] Integration is not merely connecting the data sources to the data repositories in your model. There exists an intermediary phase of data cleansing and data staging.

Reporting Phase

Reporting is sometimes the least noted and the most important part of the exercise. BSC projects have stumbled because models were built with little testing as to whether certain reports could be developed from them. There are several ways to report your findings to management:

- Use the built-in reports in BSC engines.
- Use OLAP (on-line analytical processing) navigation engines to build software reports that you can drill down into.
- Use report mining[6] systems that trigger reports on certain predetermined high and low water marks of performance.
- User custom reports generated by your staff.
- User Web-based HTML reports that can be posted regularly for review.

Data- and Measures-Replenishment Phase

Collecting information from individuals is easy the first time. They are as excited about the mystery of BSC as you are. They may spend hours being asked questions about the work they perform. Much time can be spent in data and information gathering the first time, but patience runs dry the second and third times. If your project is continuous and information on data and the structure of your activities changes, data gathering is a challenge. Note that the more important and challenging information is not what you get from other systems. Previously, we noted that much of the model information is found "somewhere" on some system in your company. You would be surprised how much unrelated information (yet to be related) is collected. Empirical information is the challenge—that is, information found only in peoples' heads. Electronic data replenishment is composed of information found in heads as well as information that resides in systems. Both must be replenished regularly, and both require preplanning in a BSC project. Data collection systems—that is, electronic surveys or query engines—permit this. Some of these tools must accommodate to surveying many people and consolidating the information for viewing. Others gather performance data as well while still others include changes in structure and can update the model interactively.

Planning Phase: Budgeting and Forecasting

Thus far, all the work performed has served us to build model(s) of our enterprise but we are still running forward, looking backward. Any results we present will be of the past, probably of the last quarter. Decisions can be made for the next year or period using this information, but we have yet to predict the results and trend what would happen if we changed certain variables. That is fundamentally what forecasting can provide. Predictive tools are evolving in BSC. Several new advances are in the horizon and will serve the BSC market well. To mention a few:

- *What if systems.* Allowing variables in the model to be adjusted to view outcomes

- *Process simulation and modeling.* Allowing a process view with model activity data such as rates to go into a time-based simulation of the enterprise in search of impediments to the process—for example, bottlenecks

Summary

BSC projects can fail before they start just like any other methodology and business transformation practice.

How an organization can implement BSC successfully:

- Pick your team and leadership.
- Pick your target and momentum drivers.
- Sell value always.

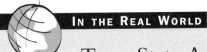

IN THE REAL WORLD

Texas State Auditor's Office
Does Lunch and Learns[a]

One of the successful implementations of Balanced Scorecard is at the Texas State Auditor's Office. How did they get started in gaining traction? After Larry Alwin, Texas state auditor, decided it was time to update his office's performance measurement system, Deborah Kerr, Alwin's chief strategy officer, became interested in scorecarding. After reading a 1996 *Harvard Business Review* article, she said, "I talked to several managers about the scorecard idea and asked if they would like to get together for some 'lunch and learn' about Balanced Scorecard and measurement." The lunch group members soon became the trusted ambassadors for BSC, the meetings gained a life of their own, and the members became a self-learning group. Six years later, the nationally recognized system continues to focus the office's attention on accountability every day.

Looking back on the history of the Texas state auditor's office system, Kerr identifies eight key actions to build momentum with BSC:

❶ Get the leader on board; top leadership must support visible accountability.

❷ Get the right people, people who can make the scorecard successful and create a skunk works. Start experimenting.

❸ Build in technology. Assume it is a management tool and a key part of the management process.

❹ Remember your goal and plan, plan, plan.

❺ Get the money in the game. Put the budget into it.

❻ Communicate about the scorecard and its value. Use newsletters, management training, and presentations.

❼ It's not over when it's over. Be persistent in managing the system.

❽ Restructure meetings around the scorecard.

[a] Interviews with Dr. Deborah Kerr, chief strategy officer, Texas state auditor's office.

- Pick outside help: consultants and vendors.

- Pick your objectives and criteria for success.

- Identify corporate strategy and thrusts.

- Build the strategy maps.

- Identify drivers and performance metrics of the perspectives.

- Identify the technology platform.

- Systematize feedback.

- Present the report-out meeting and your communications strategy.

- Win the right to do it all over again.

What is a sample road map to the activities that must be performed around a BSC system?

- Objectives-setting phase

- Data-gathering phase

- Modeling and performance-measurement-design phase

- Integrating phase

- Reporting phase

- Data- and measures-replenishment phase

- Planning phase—budgeting and forecasting

CHAPTER 9

Success Factor Four: Treat Balanced Scorecard as a Project

 After reading this chapter, you will be able to

- Treat a BSC exercise as a project using project management fundamentals and product introduction skills.

- Understand why the needs of users increase.

- Define a project schedule with deliverables.

- Identify overall project guidelines and system design.

- Develop a set of deliverables in a phased approach to the BSC project.

- Define the level of involvement for each consultant and vendor.

- Build and manage a performance measures dictionary.

- Establish a tools inventory.

B SC projects need strict and controlled sequencing. Without disciplined management and leadership, projects tend to be overcommitted, understaffed, and miscalculated. As Brent Lank from Subaru-Isuzu Automative Inc., said, "Our first thought was to do this all at one time, plant-wide. However, with what little intelligence I'm credited on having, I knew it would end up being an overwhelming activity." His team developed a project plan, and built the project throughout their thirty sections and departments.[1] Planning overcomes failure, and this chapter provides general examples and samples of technology project management. Managing a BSC project should be looked upon as managing a product development and introduction cycle rather than just project management. If implementation teams view the introduction of BSC like the introduction of a new service offering to new clients, projects would take a more effective turn. If project leaders view their challenge in this way, they would understand and take into account these various aspects:

- Messaging
- Expectation setting
- Project management and communication
- Periodic reporting
- The formalisms of periodic deliverables and written plans that culminate in an effective introduction into the target audience

A project and product focused BSC program would do the following:

- Assume that the needs of users will always increase.
- Define a project schedule with deliverables.
- Identify overall project phases and conceptual system design.
- Develop a detailed set of deliverables and assign owners in each phase of the project.
- Define the levels of involvement of consultants and vendors.
- Manage your activity dictionary.
- Establish a tools inventory.

Needs of Users Will Always Increase

Projects must be defined and stakes placed firmly in the ground. If not, requirements will increase faster than any implementation can catch them. If the project succeeds, the expectations will increase as well. A survey by Atre Associates showed that many datamarts were built in three to four months and grew at 100 percent or more yearly. This led Atre Associates to postulate that pilot projects, without much additional functions, become the production system.[2] A project-planning document should define the scope of the project but also highlight the depth of future implementations to ward off the challenges that tend to be placed on a project. This phase is similar to the requirements phase described in Chapter 8, but the scope of this document is wider because it should cover more than just the model architecture. BSC programs tend to focus on building the strategy map or getting the data into the models or building the scorecards. These are all tactical project items that forget the processes and management that must go into making BSC a part of organizational life. It should address various aspects of the project such as resources needed, ongoing training and development, schedule issues, timelines, and expected results.

Define a Project Schedule with Deliverables

Exhibit 9.1 illustrates a sample project schedule with timelines and deliverables. Traditional Gantt charting is appropriate. A BSC project could be enabled by treating it as a product introduction. Here, the rigorous demands of project and product management take hold. Exhibit 9.2 drives this home with three separate views of the same project:

1. Phases view

2. Activities view

3. Documentation view

Each view brings out a different yet significant view of the same project. Once a project outlines all the checks and balances in each view, the project begins to form three dimensionally.

EXHIBIT 9.1

Timeline Examples

	OCT	NOV	DEC	JAN	FEB
Initial Phase 1: **Technology Implementation** • Site 1 • Site 2	▬	▬	▬		
Phase 2: **Technology Implementation in All Sites** • Site 1 • Sites 2 to 5 • Includes data-gathering phases	▬	▬	▬	▬	
Final Report and **Future Enhancement Report** • Training and technology updating			▬	▬	
Phase 3: **Global Implementation** • Training of sites • Rapid prototyping session • Model development • Multisite reporting calendar			▬	▬	▬

Project Views

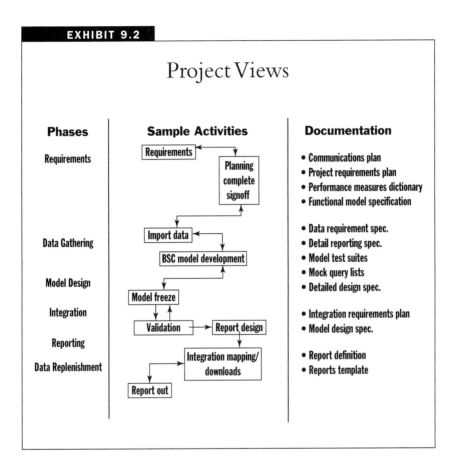

Phases   **Sample Activities**   **Documentation**

Identify Overall Project Schedules and Systems Design

Management will not deal with complexity well. BSC teams must first boil down all their activities into a few key phases. Exhibit 9.3 is an example of the five basic phases that can be used to stage a pilot project schedule to management. Exhibit 9.4 is an example of a conceptual design identifying the inputs to the system, the outputs of the system, and the system repositories and data staging centers to prepare and format information.

Maps like this remove many doubts on why, where, and what is needed to build strategy maps, scorecards, performance measures, and models that hold them.

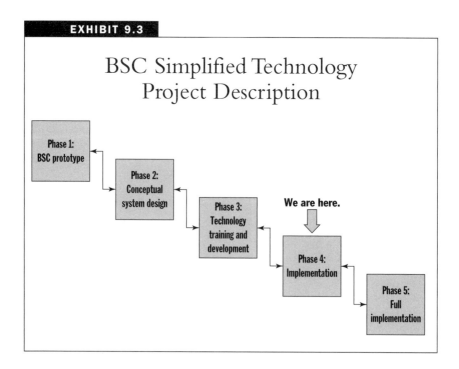

EXHIBIT 9.3

BSC Simplified Technology Project Description

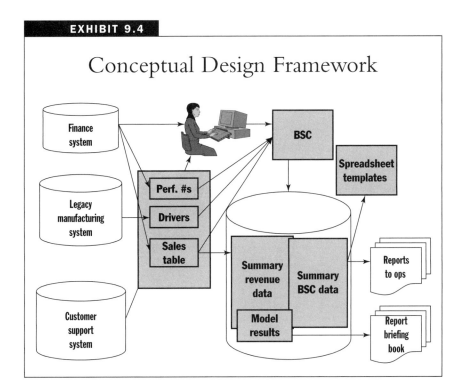

EXHIBIT 9.4

Conceptual Design Framework

TIPS & TECHNIQUES

How Fast Can You Get a Project Done at First Implementation?

If the project plan is complete; the software is in place; the performance indicators and measures are established, it could go relatively quickly. But be careful. Speeding up the cycle of learning and development for the team and the rest of the organization sometimes means that the project has made quick decisions to prove a point of the project rather than to establish the underpinnings of lasting change. Projects that "blast" through the fundamentals make strong assumptions and take risks, which can work as in the abovementioned example. However, the development of the project is less important to the development of the competency within the organization.

Tips & Techniques continued

Consider the following checks and balances in project progress:

- Has the change team learned?
- Can the pilot program be scaled, and in what timeframe?
- Will the key members of the team remain if asked to do this full-time? Or are they burned-out?
- What are the resources that go into a full-production environment, and how much time would be taken to retrace steps already taken in haste?
- Can we recruit members to the team and not have them trained because they already have learned from the process?

Develop a Detailed Set of Deliverables and Assign Owners to Each Phase of the Project

Exhibit 9.5 illustrates sample deliverables in each phase of the pilot. These outputs are critical to the success of the project. Mini-milestones within each project phase will alleviate the sense of hopelessness that overcomes any project team viewing the project as a whole. It is said that if you measure by the minute, you will slip by the minute; if you measure by the month, you will slip by the month.

EXHIBIT 9.5

Preliminary Schedule Sample

Task	Responsibility	Target Date	Actual Date
Kick-off project team.			
Rapid prototyping class			
Draft project plan.			
Complete BSC model: • Create measures dictionary. • Create perspectives with strategic themes. • Create linkage to downstream measures. • Create strategy map. • Develop communication plan.			
Define and generate reports.			
Update lifecycle documents.			
BSC team review of update			
Management review			
Incorporate feedback from management.			
Review security design.			
Import GL/sales measures information.			
Import manufacturing measures information.			
Manager review			
Develop reports			
Present results to management team.			

Define the Level of Involvement for Each Consultant and Vendor

BSC projects can be complex challenges if the roles of consultants, vendors, and the in-house teams are not defined. Up front, successful program leaders identify the required functions for each of the players and then manage their effectiveness. Exhibit 9.6 illustrates such a mapping for a project. Once this responsibility chart is drawn, any resource mix-ups or role misunderstanding will be identified. Also, resource problems will be brought out in the beginning of the process. Some BSC projects have lasted so long that the staff on the project leaves or changes. It is very im-

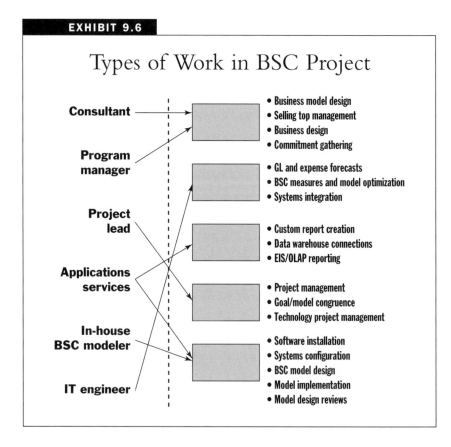

Types of Work in BSC Project

Consultant
- Business model design
- Selling top management
- Business design
- Commitment gathering

Program manager
- GL and expense forecasts
- BSC measures and model optimization
- Systems integration

Project lead
- Custom report creation
- Data warehouse connections
- EIS/OLAP reporting

Applications services
- Project management
- Goal/model congruence
- Technology project management

In-house BSC modeler
- Software installation
- Systems configuration
- BSC model design

IT engineer
- Model implementation
- Model design reviews

portant to know the level of contribution and participation demanded of each member so that resources can be brought in to fill the need.

Manage Your Dictionary

Many BSC projects end before they begin. These projects tend to manage using all the sophisticated technology, strong management support, and project management but still stumble. The secret ingredient seems less process-oriented than content-specific. The use of a dictionary is critical to establishing the language of the project. Exhibit 9.7 illustrates a sample page in a dictionary for performance measures. Similar dictionaries must be created for all other aspects of endeavor so that organizational memory does not fade. Note that it describes the nature of the performance measure—that is, leading/lagging, its source, the activity it supports, its members, its process parents, inputs, the type of its measure, and possible target measures, among others. Further additions include when and how to collect its data.

EXHIBIT 9.7

Performance Measures Dictionary Item Sample

Performance dictionary #:	Owner:
Performance measure type: Leading/lagging indicator: Target: Measure: Other attributes:	Description: Comments: Period: Source data:
Strategic theme: Objective:	Linked with and to:
Why is this measure important?	

A performance measures dictionary isolates the more important contents of the BSC model prior to beginning the project. This may seem tedious initially as it may seem that the momentum of the project is compromised when everyone sits in a room defining activities. The value of this exercise will only show itself later in the project.

Establish a Tools Inventory

Just as a map defines a landscape, a *tools schematic* topologically identifies the necessary tools/solutions the project will use. Exhibit 9.8 illustrates such a topological view of tools. Alternative tools could also assist your project and safeguard technology crises that may surface. If alternatives are identified, the project must ensure that data models can be converted prior to the development start.

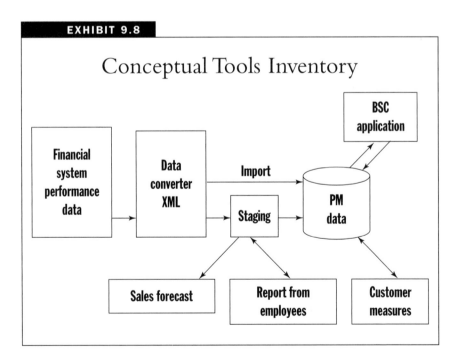

EXHIBIT 9.8

Conceptual Tools Inventory

IN THE REAL WORLD

Regence Group Takes the Right Perspective

The Regence Group combined five separate businesses under one umbrella several years ago. Each operation ran under its own management and board but under the guide of The Regence Group.

The group experienced difficulties in its initial years in aligning authority, accountability, and roles in executing toward a vision. It realized a key problem was the lack of a single strategy to guide the combined enterprise. It undertook a business transformation process. Balanced Scorecard was a key tool for implementing it.

BSC was the obvious tool to align each organization under a strategic umbrella. The executive team directed a team to research and understand the value proposition offered by a BSC implementation. The team researched the issues and proposed their ideas to the management team, who then instructed the team to go forward. BSC could have taken on a life of its own then.

Realizing that BSC can function only when a strong strategic direction has been established, Mark Ganz, CEO of The Regence Group, instituted a strategic planning process to identify key strategic thrusts that are now the key feeders into the BSC process.

Summary

Treat a BSC exercise as a project using project management. If an organization begins a BSC exercise with a one-time-only mentality, the project will never take off. In fact, the project team will inherently believe in relief and will cut corners to ensure success. This will only push off big decisions and mortgage the future for the present. It might be good to consider this BSC program as one would view the education and introduction of a new product that has customers to satisfy, engineering to educate and guide, and sales to ensure revenue. This mentality could remind the team that they serve, not institute, change and that they must constantly sell their ideas and their product.

The best sign of a successful BSC program is when the audience asks for more and more adjustments. This is not a bad sign because only users ask for more. The BSC exercise is a project-planning exercise and a market-introduction exercise rolled into one. Hence, using project scheduling, deliverable planning, and overall guidelines of project management, BSC will live. The use of consultants and other outside help is not all bad, but one must ensure that they are carefully guided and rewarded.

CHAPTER 10

Success Factor Five: Use Technology as an Enabler

After reading this chapter, you will be able to

- Recognize three classes of BSC systems.
- Understand common subsystems of any BSC system.
- Decide which software vendor to work with.

As discussed earlier, there are three main aspects to any business transformation:

1. People issues

2. Process issues

3. Technology issues

This chapter deals with the technology issues even though the people and process issues cannot be separated from this discussion. There are several overlaps as people implement technology and process enables technology.

Three classes of BSC systems exist:

1. One that is integrated into legacy and accounting systems—called enterprise performance management (EPM) systems or enterprise resource planning (ERP) systems

2. One that is best-of-breed analytic application used alongside integrated enterprise system—called analytic applications or business intelligence applications

3. An in-house designed-and-built system—called internally developed applications

In all these systems, the following subsystems must exist for the correct delivery of an effective BSC system (see Exhibit 10.1):

- Data collection and input subsystem
- Modeling and analysis subsystem
- Reporting subsystem
- Deployment subsystem
- Predictive and planning subsystem
- Infrastructure subsystem

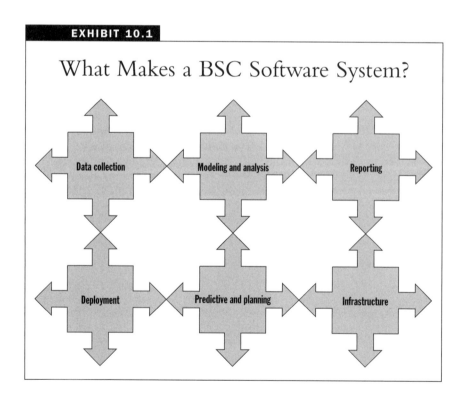

EXHIBIT 10.1

What Makes a BSC Software System?

Data Collection and Input Subsystem

The importance of data collection is only understood after the first BSC exercise. At the pilot, the information gathered through interviews, combined with tapping ASCII (text-based) data dumps from heterogeneous databases, seems trivial. The initial excitement in the organization and hence, its openness to cooperate, is high. Everyone is willing to spend time and money on a first try. Everyone is also willing to hardcode the connections with data and not wonder what to do when the data structures change. One good side effect to finding out where the performance measures reside is that more often than not, there is more than one location where the same data lives. Consolidating these locations into one can "save untold dollars spent on entering data in several locations," as Subaru-Isuzu Automotive Inc. discovered.[1]

When repeated data and structures of the model must be replenished continuously, the real challenge to the maintainability of the system surfaces. Many BSC systems provide data collection tools that provide electronic data replenishment (EDR) tools, that is, tools designed to assist in repeated data collection of performance information that is found in multiple sources including data found in peoples' heads.

EDR is not focused on collecting data for the first time. Many other methods and systems allow for this. The biggest challenge in data collection is in data replenishment, that is, gathering data the second and third time from the same people. Data can be transaction information but also information found in peoples' heads; empirical information is essential to the process. BSC projects, using technology, can gather information found on systems, but empirical information must be gathered using online surveys or with interviews. Exhibit 10.2 illustrates this variety of information-gathering methods, pushed into a Balanced Scorecard datawarehouse or a navigations engine.

EXHIBIT 10.2

Trade–Offs of Each Data Source Gathering

Interfaces	Purpose	Advantages	Disadvantages	Comments
ASCII	Importing, exporting ASCII data files are input in specified format.	Quick access. Simple interface, and defined among many software packages.	One time only. It must take all the ASCII data like a spoon takes food.	
ODBC Query	Standards-based query engine can grab information selectively, like chopsticks can pick food items.	Very directed and selective connection to data. Very scripted and repeatable.	Must learn the query engine language.	
Web-Based Survey Tools	Empirical knowledge; that is, information not found on systems can be captured.	Gets to information found in peoples' heads, not systems. Is anonymous, and increases data correctness. Repeatable and measurable because you can find out how	Must understand another feature of the system to collect information. Surveys can be intimidating to noncomputer-literate users and might not get all the salient effects	

			derived from eye-to-eye interviews.
		many really responded and urge more response. Less time-consuming than interviews.	
Spreadsheet	Simple input mechanics.	Nonintimidating input and output. Graphical connections are known and understood.	Too simple. Cannot collect vast amount of data because spreadsheet runs out of steam with limited storage capabilities. Data collection is unidimensional unless you spend time to create multiple dimensions.
XML-Based Query Methods	eXtensible Markup Language devised to create a standard method for applications to speak with each other.	Becoming a strong standard in the industry for application developers. Highly efficient way to grab data from various data sources.	Requires technical expertise to understand the language formats. May not be applicable for legacy systems.

Input and output subsystems take the following forms:

- ASCII importing and exporting
- Object data-base connectivity (ODBC) connections with a query engine (EDR tools)
- Survey-like Web-based input and output systems (EDR tools)
- XML[2] (eXtensible Markup Language) data interfaces.

Some installations have several connections to heterogeneous performance data sources. In certain organizations the data are found only in peoples' heads. Service companies, for example, tend to have time information but not to have performance information logged in systems. Manufacturing companies who have systems tend to have some manufacturing-related information on-line and might only have them handled on the shop floor. Data collection can be vast or targeted. All this depends on the expanse of the BSC model being created. If you have 1,000 objectives and 400 performance measures with 2,000 initiatives, it will take more time in setting up systems versus populating 10 objectives, 19 performance measures, and so on. In the case of the Canadian Department of Defense, in particular the Army of the Canadian Forces, its software, Panorama Business Views, a BSC vendor, was set up to cover the following:

- 4 organizational levels of management[3]
- 250 users in 200 locations
- 1,289 measures feeding 35 indicators per scorecard

Exhibit 10.3 shows the various data sources and the tools that can connect them into the BSC datawarehouse.

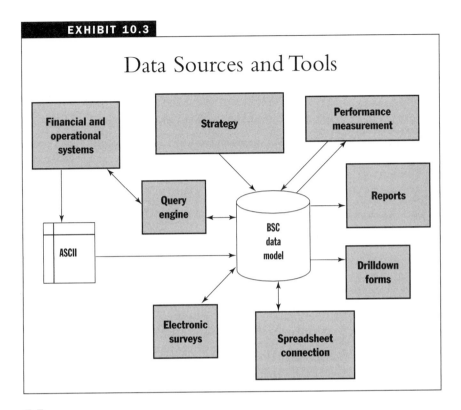

EXHIBIT 10.3

Data Sources and Tools

Modeling and Analysis Subsystem

In order for a thorough capture and evaluation of the strategic drivers of an enterprise, a periodic snapshot of the flow of key strategic objectives and its associated performance measures is essential and forms the basic foundation for the development of a BSC model.

As discussed in prior chapters, many organizations are satisfied with strategy modeling at first but very quickly realize that their model needs to be extended to measure costs and include revenue, profits, and a host of other objectives and measures. Some associate the model as a measurement backbone for other initiatives or other measurement subsystems.

For example, organizations might relate EVA (economic value added)[4] to activity-based costing (ABC) or total quality management (TQM) projects, often wishing to uncover deeper analysis from the scorecard.

Hence, BSC systems can take a deeper role than basic scorecarding of performance management elements. In a nutshell, the modeling and analysis subsystem can create several views of the objectives, initiatives, measures, targets, and metrics data:

- The classic BSC framework with its performance measurements

- The process views showing the relationship of activities to each other and their parents—namely, tasks and processes

- The multidimensional views such as profitability by channel or by product or many more—a "slice and dice" model often called OLAP and popularized by companies like Cognos Corp.

- The scorecard view that uses this base to reflect performance metrics held by the organization

Reporting and Deployment Subsystems

BSC teams gain an enormous understanding of their own company from the inside out and begin to ask the questions that place them on the road to improvement. BSC helps frame the corporate strategy.

Key to this learning is the "Report-out" meeting held to impress the management of findings. All multifunction project teams conclude their work with presentations. These presentations report on the model's output and response to queries about the work performed. These meetings seem always to come too early. Many a sleepless night is spent to win in these presentations, and the emotions of all concerned are high.

Reporting subsystems are critical at this moment. They produce two-dimensional reports with graphs that bring the entire data gathering, modeling, and analysis exercise into perspective.

Today there are two ways to report on the project data:

1. *Built-in reports from the software.* Custom reports designed specific to the special organization expectation. Some custom report writers also have a built-in query engine that grabs information just as a data collection engine does. These engines allow for custom reports to be built through the design of reports with links to data elements within the BSC model. Then, anytime you want a report to update you on the status of the information, just run the engine. Furthermore, enhancement to this approach touches the fields of data mining—often called *report mining*. Here, scripts can be set up to awaken the query engine, interrogate the models, and invoke the reporting subsystem when certain data triggers occur—that is, if a measure exceeds $5 million for product X. Exhibit 10.4 illustrates such a configuration for report mining.

EXHIBIT 10.4

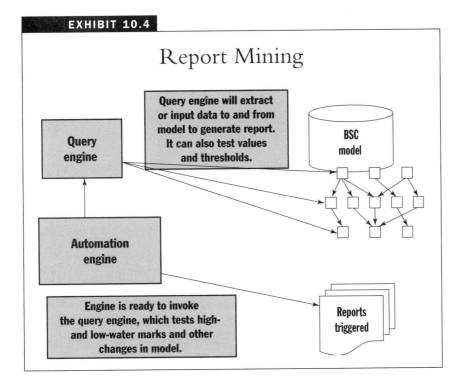

Report Mining

Query engine will extract or input data to and from model to generate report. It can also test values and thresholds.

Query engine

BSC model

Automation engine

Engine is ready to invoke the query engine, which tests high- and low-water marks and other changes in model.

Reports triggered

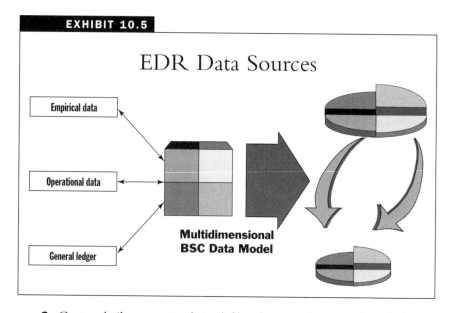

EXHIBIT 10.5

EDR Data Sources

Empirical data

Operational data

General ledger

**Multidimensional
BSC Data Model**

2. *Custom-built, computer-derived files that permit personal, multidimensional computer investigation by management.* Each file uses data navigation software to drill down and analyze the data. These tools are also called executive information systems (EIS) or business intelligence (BI). Being a refreshing adjunct to flat reporting, these tools permit the user to interrogate the data and navigate through a succession of graphs, drilling down to uncover the true causes or other dimensions in their model. See Exhibit 10.5.

Predictive and Planning Subsystems

C. J. McNair, professor of management accounting at Babson College, states, "Knowing the score isn't the goal—changing it is."[5] In the end, it's not the information on your desktop that is key; it's the accuracy, timeliness, and the applicability of the decisions you make from it. With BSC, managers no longer deal with the present using data from the past. Inherently, they all want to predict the future. Thus far, the tools available to them have been limited and not everyone has the time, the training, or the energy to develop elaborate models of reality.

However, the BSC framework provides some strong insight to perform predictions and planning. BSC, being an umbrella to the overall performance framework of an organization, can frame the performance data and consolidate information from many other analytic application data repositories, such as the following:

- Activity-based budgeting
- Cost management systems
- Sales reporting systems
- Manufacturing process management systems
- Claims management systems
- Target costing
- Process measurement and tracking—time-based simulations
- Capacity planning
- Yield analysis and predictions
- What-if analysis

All of these opportunities for further analysis can be reflected from any BSC system under the predictive subsystem.

Infrastructure Subsystem

In more advanced BSC systems, infrastructure holds disparate tools in place and permits the user(s) to manage the information flow through them. Infrastructure controls the licenses in the toolset and restricts access at various levels of the software. Some packages are stand-alone PC-tools; others are LAN or enterprise-based (local area network) network accessible frameworks that hold and monitor access to tools.

Issues of security, licensing, and network capabilities are key concerns to most corporate system administrators and IT professionals. No two BSC systems are built alike with the same administrative paradigm in mind. They must always be built on general-purpose computing environments, and your IT-professional can assist you in that diagnosis.

One way to get a start on this is to ask the following questions:

- How do I plan on using this information system, that is, from my computer or on a network?

- How many people must have access to the system, and at which phases of the project?

- What are the key tools I will need to get the job done?

- Who will maintain and help me fix problems within my company?

- Do I need this tool to be a client-server? LAN-based network? Or stand-alone?

Virtual Nature of Subsystems

These subsystems can exist on multiple systems with heterogeneous base architectures and databases. For example, the organization may have an EPM that handles BSC, product-costing, and operational reporting, while certain elements of ABC modeling and profitability modeling are handled by an off-line, connected PC-based system. Technology and methodology have advanced to a level where the physical location of an application is secondary to the functionality of the application environment. Hence, the location of applications can be less important to the work. New architectures are evolving to support the key managerial processes like BSC and are becoming less of the main challenge.

Deciding Which Software Vendor to Work With

Every datasheet tells the same story but is equally exaggerated. Ever visit a tradeshow? After a short while on the tradeshow floor, all the products and all the sales people look like they work for the same organization, don't they? They seem to say all the same phrases and deny all the same accusations. Everyone seems to be the "market leader," "dominant," "high performance," and "undisputed choice."

The key questions still remain in the exercise of making the purchase decision:

- How does an organization truly differentiate one from another?
- How does an organization purchase one package and vendor and adjust as the needs of the organization change?
- What do I do if my consultant recommends a vendor against my own instincts?

Rules of Engagement in Understanding a Vendor

Clearly, no two software vendors have the same personality. They are different from the way they build software to the way they market them. There are nine rules of engagement that can assist in comparing and understanding vendors in the analytic BSC environment. The following nine rules of engagement serves to assist in evaluating a BSC software provider:

1. Understand organizational needs.
2. Make a rational decision using a process with checklists and reviews.
3. Evaluate more than software.
4. Don't use the vendors to learn BSC exclusively.
5. Visit your vendors and tour.
6. Don't get caught in trends.
7. Always keep in touch with the market.
8. The nature of the dance is the nature of the relationship. Watch and measure all aspects of the relationship with the vendor.
9. Control the demonstration.

Understand Organizational Needs

If you don't know beauty, then everyone looks beautiful. Understanding your needs and also your ability to absorb your needs are the keys to any process of evaluating and working with others. Many BSC projects start on the wrong foot—lack of planning around the demands of the organization. There are several questions to ponder:

- Does the organizational team agree that the tools to be purchased cannot substitute the process and people issues to be tackled?

- What portion of data gathering does the team believe is manual or computer controlled?

- What can the team and organization absorb in terms of sophisticated software modules?

- Is the organization technology-averse and demanding of technology?

- What kind of User interface works for the extended organization?

- What data management requirements are anticipated and can the internal IT groups support the system?

Make a Rational Decision Using a Process with Checklists and Reviews

The team evaluating these vendors must understand the priorities of these needs and the appropriate trade-off your management team and you are willing to discuss. Even though compromise is the essence of the evaluation process, a haphazard, gut-feel approach will give room for errors in judgment. Without a practical process to guide your evaluation, emotion, bureaucracy, politics, and irrational conjecture will flood your decision-making system. The following suggestions are for selecting the vendor:

- Select a team to perform the selection.
- Establish agreed-upon timelines for the requirements development, the request for proposal formats, meeting times, decision processes, and the vendors that are on the list.
- Determine key criteria needed to select the candidate vendors.

Evaluate More Than Software

There are few barriers to entry in software. All it takes is an office, software engineers, and a phone to bring a software company to life. Great software companies are more than this. They are systems built to carry you through the hard times and to support you through your growing needs for results. In your evaluation, consider that you are not evaluating a product or a service but a new alliance with a company that has proposed to serve you. Software is changing all the time, and as you assess the use of any software package, you should assess the relationship you will be having with the respective organization. Recognizing that software is only the device part of the product, other components are brought together to make the product whole:

- The service component
- The support infrastructure
- The company itself, the relationship your company can count on
- The financial infrastructure backing the company, and so on

Don't Use the Vendors to Learn BSC Exclusively

In many demo situations, clients ask basic questions about BSC and how it can be applied. Software vendors will always educate you about the industry and the market, but for one reason—you buy their solution. It is important that the purchasing organization rely on more than vendor knowledge to accelerate the project.

Most software vendors are trained to educate you on the subject, but to also set the barriers in features and benefits against their competitors. The under-educated client could be led astray following a vendor's agenda.

In these demo circumstances, you must ensure that your team is well versed with the requirements and with the expectations of a meeting. Software vendors are useful learning resources, but they should not be the sole source of your education. Your organization should develop a model for educating itself prior to the demo.

Visit Your Vendors and Tour

Software and systems vendors who are proud of their growth and want to take advantage of their reputation will share everything about themselves. They tend to invite you to visit their offices and tour their facilities. Many BSC software vendors are smaller and tend to work out of smaller offices. Others are really sales offices with research and development overseas. It is important to meet the customer support professionals who will help your when the going gets tough. Furthermore, you must understand their quality-assurance procedures, if any. This could save you from disaster.

Before you go on the trip, make sure to do the following:

- Set the agenda and meet senior management.

- Present your strategy to them and make them accountable to your needs.

- Observation skills must be used during a tour, for example, observe their sales organization and see if they are busy.

- Talk to the engineers and ask them BSC questions.

- Find out how many are working on your product purchase.

- Visit the office of your sales representative and see what the rep's environment is in the hierarchy of sales.

All in all, the best way to pick a vendor is to visit one. Then move from vendor-client relationships to a partnership.

Don't Get Caught in Trends

Many BSC projects are change-management projects. Visionaries lead these projects, and they are filled with the endorphins of possibilities. This is a needed characteristic for dramatic change. However, the very characteristics that change agents possess can be the source of their downfall if not held in check.

In the early phases of a project, the appetites of organizations are large and their digestive systems seem to have the unlimited capacity for technology adoption.

Trends in new advances can only accentuate our addictions for technology. These are valuable technologies of the future but note that one cannot build tomorrow on tomorrow's technology. One can only build tomorrow on today's technology. Hence, test the ability of the vendor to be honest and direct about what has been tested and works versus what is being tried on your organization.

Always Keep in Touch with the Market

Loyalty is a virtue. In BSC projects, the risk of implementation is inherently high and sometimes loyalty to one vendor can be a mistake. Generally, almost 50 percent of technology implementations fail to meet expectations. One way to prevent any setbacks in the technology elements of the project is to hedge your bets by creating alternatives to your technical implementation. Portability of your modeling environment requires that you examine more than one vendor and keep them close at hand in case trouble brews.

Keeping multiple seconds and one loyal partner is difficult, especially since you have trained all your people on a certain technology. The one

TIPS & TECHNIQUES

Remember the Ten Questions

The following ten questions will help profile a BSC vendor.

❶ Is the BSC vendor more than a one-product company or a one-product group with no diversity in its BSC offering?

❷ Is the BSC vendor a software company or a consulting firm in disguise?

❸ How large is the vendor's installed base in BSC?

❹ Does the vendor support the BSC products with training and technical services?

❺ Does the vendor have support of an active, international user group? Does the vendor have regional BSC user group meetings?

❻ Does the BSC product adhere to industry standards?

❼ Does the BSC product support an open standards-based interface?

❽ Does the BSC product have a technical and feature migration path?

❾ Does the BSC product support an interface to other productivity tools like process modeling, activity-based costing?

❿ Does the BSC vendor support an integrated BSC environment?

great advantage is the standards that have been built around BSC, and this will assist in portability and redundancy.

The Nature of the Dance Is the Nature of the Relationship: Watch All Aspects of the Relationship

The customer–vendor courtship is much like a marriage courtship. Obviously, the first date is a wonderful experience for many, but can it last? Through this courtship, you will come to understand the style of your prospective partner and how they view a partnership.

Some vendors like selling futures, while others only sell the present and never talk about the future. Others are hungry enough to work with you regularly while others will disappear when the purchase order is cut. Some keep commitments while others promise but deliver late. Do you want someone who accepts your idiosyncrasies or one who challenges them?

Throughout the process of meeting, understanding, and purchasing software for BSC, your organization must assess the value and the future of the partnership. As we all know, partnerships are always deemed to be strategic even when they are merely tactical and short-term. So, the selection of a vendor for software must be categorized as one or the other and treated that way.

Control the Demonstration

Many demos are considered the ultimate decision point. Realistically, they are like beauty contests when they should be like fitness tests. They are staged events that make or break a sales opportunity. This emphasis may be due to the "seeing is believing" mentality in the buying process. Yet, what you see might not be what you get. Often, the software providers control demos. They follow tight and fail-safe scripted demos that highlight the power of their solution and loosen your mental grip on their competitors.

So, the ultimate lesson to learn is not to let this happen but to control the sources of information used in a demo; control the issues discussed; control the decisions to be made; and control the attendees' expectations.

If you tend to a free-form engagement of ideas and expectations, you will get exactly that—just ideas. The following checklist hints at organizing the meeting based on requirements and expectations:

- Determine the number of demos and vendors to review.
- Understand their strengths and weaknesses ahead and communicate.
- Determine the areas you want highlighted.
- Decide who should attend, and what areas they are to observe.
- Know how flexible the demo givers are to changing the issues they set.
- Measure their consistency with their literature and Web-page information.
- Ask and plan questions to be asked. The most important question to ask is about the demo givers—ask them how long they have been with the company, and the answers may surprise you.
- Provide a base model for them to build, and inject an error to observe their response.
- Provide each of the demo giver scores. If you're brave, share them with the demo givers.
- Don't react; anticipate their actions and put them into your agenda for testing.
- Respect your vendor. Above all, don't make it a selling event. Make it a dialog to understand if two mature parties can see a common future.

Summary

Technology has developed to a level where BSC can be implemented for sustainability. However, technology, like any tool, if in the hands of a knowledgeable individual, will perform. The users level of knowledge and experience defines the success criteria more than the ease of the software systems. This chapter seeks to provide a conceptual foundation for viewing systems and software. It is not focused on the details of software features and what to test for. These features will come and go over time, but the needs will remain.

Prioritizing Technology in Texas

The Texas state auditor's office (SAO) scorecard implementation team, led by Deborah Kerr (chief strategy officer), realized early in its design phase that technology would be key to the ongoing implementation. They wanted to move away from the four-inch binders full of spreadsheets to a more useful format for data presentation. After mapping the initial scorecard plan, the team concluded that it would be more cost-effective to purchase a software application than to build one in-house. The decision to adopt a technology-based process paid off. "Technology is a key part of the management process," Kerr says. "All our management reports are on-line and technology facilitates our thinking about how the organization is working."[a]

Using a request-for-proposal process, the agency used open bidding to select a vendor that met their needs. Based on the measurement system design, the selected system would have to provide:

- Capability for data comparison and data analysis
- Reporting flexibility and customization
- Ease of implementation
- Flexibility to change data items
- Internet capability, data importing, and exporting capability
- Customer support
- User-friendly interface
- Competitive pricing and good customer support[b]

[a] Based on interviews with Dr. Deborah L. Kerr, chief strategy officer, Texas state auditor's office.
[b] Deborah L. Kerr, "The Business of Government: The Balanced Scorecard in the Public Sector," *Perform Magazine* 1, no. 8 (October 2001), p. 4.

Several classes of systems exist for user selection:

- The integrated accounting systems have BSC modules.

- The smaller analytic systems dedicated to BSC also exist.

- Organizations that think the abovementioned systems are too generic tend to build their own systems.

All have their own benefits and all have drawbacks, but the key element of the decision sits with the organizational expectations, and disappointment only occurs when there is a mismatch between the needs of the users and the abilities of the systems to provide these needs. It is important to know how users will exercise the system and the processes they will undertake before selecting systems. Failure to do so will result in the systems driving the methods, rather than vice versa.

All analytic systems like BSC have six subsystems:

1. Data collection

2. Modeling and analysis

3. Reporting

4. Deployment

5. Predictive and planning

6. Infrastructure

These subsystems work in concert with each other to serve the user. Vendors have focus and emphasis on these subsystems. Furthermore, vendors must be selected on a wider horizon than just the technology. This chapter has outlined the characteristics of a good vendor, who probably displays the characteristics of a partner.

CHAPTER 11

Success Factor Six: Cascade the Scorecard

After reading this chapter, you will be able to

- See why to cascade the scorecard.
- Recognize the benefits of enterprisewide BSC.
- Understand the challenges in developing an enterprisewide BSC implementation.

P aul Niven, author of *Balanced Scorecard, Step-by Step: Maximizing Performance and Maintaining Results*, defines cascading as "the process of developing Balanced Scorecards at each and every level of your organization."[1] When cascading a scorecard, we are doing the following:

- Driving the BSC mentality and methodology deep into the fabric of the organization
- Enabling all voices to share in the orchestration of strategy
- Implementing—not technology, but through technology a new management process and habit

Cascading the scorecard is the embodiment of this intent.

Exhibit 11.1 illustrates the benefits of cascading the scorecard:

- Cascading builds *awareness* across the enterprise of the key strategies and objectives and measures the organization needs to accomplish in the attainment of the future.

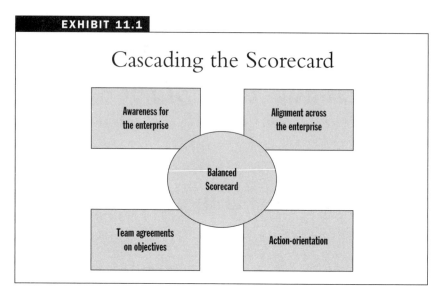

EXHIBIT 11.1

Cascading the Scorecard

Awareness for
the enterprise

Alignment across
the enterprise

Balanced
Scorecard

Team agreements
on objectives

Action-orientation

- It builds *alignment* in the organization to the main objectives and brings every member closer to the real targets, which they can participate in achieving.

- It builds *agreement* among team members across the organization when decisions are being made daily as to priorities within in the corporation or entity. Here, employees can decide very quickly if trade-offs lead to the ultimate goals and strategy attainment.

- It builds *action*-orientation when performance measures are attached to each objective and strategy. What gets measured gets done.

What Are the Benefits of Enterprise BSC?

Exhibit 11.2 illustrates the vital steps taken in the creation and deployment of a BSC methodology. This method is not a top-down process and requires the careful orchestration at all levels. Frankly, the BSC is a framework for gathering all the insights an organization can deliver to strategy. It drives the organization to focus and align all resources to the main strategic themes and to share in the win.

EXHIBIT 11.2

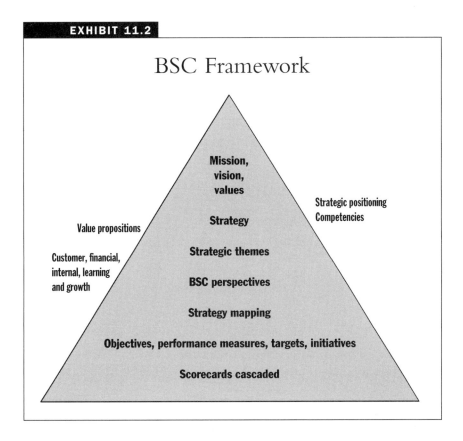

BSC Framework

The exhibit summarizes the key elements of the strategic framework as described in this book:

- Identifying the purpose of the organization with mission, vision, values

- Clarifying strategy with an eye to competencies the organization has or can attain

- Breaking strategy into key themes that the organization can absorb

- Drawing on strategy maps to understand cause-and-effect relationships between four-plus perspectives

- Developing performance measures within each perspective but also between perspectives, showing a balance of measures as well

- Building key Balanced Scorecards around each objective, sub-objectives, and initiatives

- Cascading theses objectives and initiatives with mutually organized measures to all levels of the organization to be used, shared, and evaluated on regular intervals.

Exhibits 11.3 to 11.5[2] show a cascaded scorecard and a prototype BSC system developed as an educational tool to help new users to the concepts behind BSC. Here, main objectives are now being shared with others within the organization, say in Claims organization for a health insurance provider. (Exhibit 11.3 illustrates a claims manager logging in to review the performance information for the month.)

Meanwhile, the Marketing group has formulated its objectives as a function of the overall goals of the corporation and established measures that reflect its department needs. These measures actually map to the measures of the scorecard given to them from above. These objectives meet the overall goals of the corporation and can be identified as such. Exhibit 11.4 illustrates the scorecard for the business overall with respect to the customer perspective. Now every member of the organization negotiates his or her objectives, target, and measures with the team and management, attempting to arrive at an optimal set of actions to be achieved within a period. The higher the objectives go up the value chain, the more strategic they become; however, at the lowest level (and most important) of the organization, work needs to be focused on the goals. Performance measures at this level are tactical and need very little interpretation, but they must be negotiated by each member of a team and measured.

Exhibit 11.5 illustrates a benchmarking capability in which individuals can view how their team or they have performed with respect to peers within and sometimes outside the organization.

EXHIBIT 11.3

Secure Log-In to the Performance Viewer

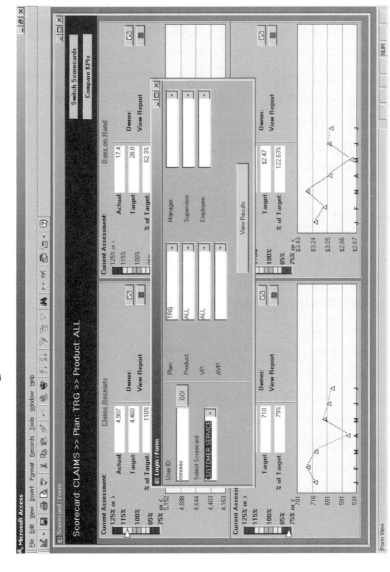

Source: Printed with permission from The Regence Group, 2003.

View the Performance Measures

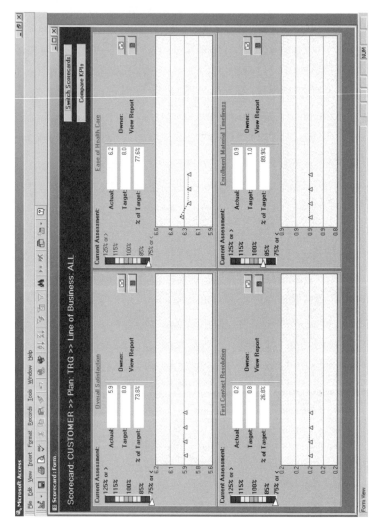

Source: Printed with permission from The Regence Group, 2003.

Benchmark Your Performance against Others

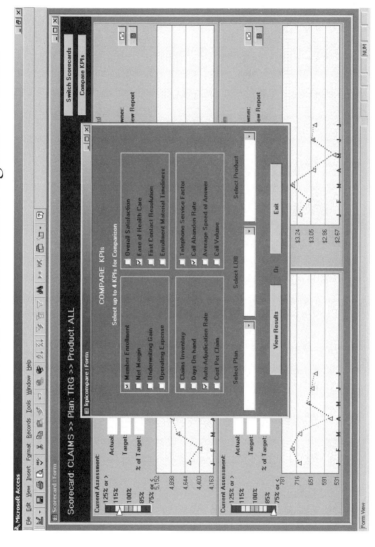

Source: Printed with permission from The Regence Group, 2003.

TIPS & TECHNIQUES

Bringing scorecards to the organization can be very intimidating because they symbolize accountability with a lack of authority. It is critical that an enterprisewide education, deployment, and sustaining plan be clear and explanatory among the management of the corporation. Merely driving a scorecard without all the supporting educational and training systems would destroy the real intent behind the scorecard. Given the positive intent, consider the following ways to get the message out and the behavior into alignment:

- *Communicate, communicate, communicate.* All managers must be trained on the purpose and the use of BSC. They can then become evangelists to this transformation and coaches to the process. Create forums for discussion and make it a priority.

- *Use it.* Use the information and the framework for discussion within key meetings and establish this scorecard in the key operational meetings so that it is a part of the habit of business.

- *Use technology.* Technology is there when you are not. One company has its scorecards come up on every computer in the morning. This forces everyone to understand the priorities daily. Technology is the tool of continuity but not the source. Leaders make technology work, and BSC depends on the focus of management.

- *Break barriers.* In my organization, I tried to convince all the individuals and teams to define, maintain, and measure accomplishment with scorecards. I spent five years convincing them, and after that, I insisted on the method and asked them to leave if they just were not going to be part of the solution. Barriers can come in the form of people, process, and technology. Ensure that these barriers are educated in or escorted out.

- *Never forget the reason behind the BSC.* If the original intent for BSC is strategic alignment to the tactics, then keep the purpose in mind always. It is very easy to forget the true purpose for which BSC was started. For example, BSC can degrade into an enterprise of pure measurement and punishment if not monitored.

What Are the Challenges in Cascading the Scorecard?

At each phase of a BSC project, threats visit at the transition from pilot to production or from production to global distribution. As in a relay race, the entire race is lost not in the running but in the passing of the baton to the next runner. Expanding the enterprisewide system implementation has similar hand-off challenges.

A few critical hints against such hindrances are:

- Design the team for enterprise expansion.
- Expand the model control technology.
- Assemble the right team again.

Design BSC for Enterprise Expansion

Organizations walk the fine line between absolute control to absolute freedom in managing and implementing global sites. BSC for the enterprise expansion suffers from a similar challenge, that is, do you control the BSC expansion with fixed rules from one location, or do you give control to sites all over the world and have little consolidation capability and viewing? Is the philosophy centralized or decentralized, or probably something in between? What does the organization want as a standard, and if this is insisted on, would the organization lose the true value of diversity and creativity? Here are some other possible issues:

- What interfaces does the organization use in technically automating the process? What standards for information transfer across multiple locations exist?
- What level of integration is expected in various sites and do they have the same technical capabilities?
- Is the knowledge and skill up to par? Do they vary from site to site?

- How do different sites change their models or increase their expectations? Is there a change process that must be approved by the central controlling body?

- Are all implementations at the same level?

TIPS & TECHNIQUES

Consider the following practice for cascading BSC:

- Start with a steering team that can manage the entire education and rollout of BSC.

- Develop training materials as well as a communication kit for all senior managers who must communicate the value and the intent behind BSC.

- Use standard performance dictionaries to ensure that all locations adhere to certain standards. Cultural variations surely exist, but make these part of an exception list.

- Deploy an internal companywide user group so that regular events are scheduled to share learning and enthusiasm.

Many organizations that wish to expand beyond their local sites to multiple BSC endeavors worldwide should consider forming internal competency centers to dispense and distribute learning and technology. These centers are responsible for the following:

- Educating users and training them
- Ensuring design and implementation consistencies
- Providing central technical support
- Selecting software and negotiating software contracts
- Being a clearinghouse for upgrades and updates of software
- Certifying model architectures and model consistencies

Expand the BSC Model and Performance Measurement Control Methodology

Enterprise deployment objectives usually include two goals:

1. *Model consolidation*

   - Model globalization
   - Roll-up of tactical models into a strategic model
   - Year-to-date consolidation from several single period models

2. *Modeling to corporate standards*

   - Checking compliance to allow consistent reporting
   - Establishing template models

Inherently, most global-enterprise rollouts encounter the following resistances:

- Tight control of model creation is resisted by local organizations.
- Complete control of local models is unnecessary and removes local cultural contribution.
- Compliance checking must be simple and painless for the local modeler.
- Standards can be easily created using common and understandable tools.

Available technology allows for consolidating models and establishing standards. In the case of model consolidation, technology now enables BSC model elements to be linked together between models. *Model linking*, as it is called, links performance measures and perspectives across models and simplifies model consolidation considerably. Client-server or XML-based (eXtensible Markup Language) technologies can help in model consolidation needs because there might be only one master model, but this architecture may create further challenges as a certain amount of a distributed computing environment increases redundancy, which might not be all that bad. A distributed computing environment, where models are part of a whole but perform independently, reduces the risk of putting all eggs in one BSC model. BSC model certification and verification ensures that models created in various sites live within certain communicated and agreed-on guidelines.

IN THE REAL WORLD

Triquint Semiconductor
Strategy Journey

In 1994, Steve Sharp, then CEO of Triquint Semiconductor, focused on developing and articulating strategy with the sole purpose of establishing strategy at all levels of the organization. He states, "If everybody does not participate, they don't get the vision."[a] Using classic SWOT[b] analysis, along with creating strategic templates for measuring performance for the long-term, Sharp drove the company's measurement system design. At first, he thought, "I did not think we needed one. My vision was clear to me!" But he wanted a "unifying effect" to this process. The great benefits came when key initiatives were uncovered:

- Re-examine selling channels
- Figure out the China market
- Understand emerging market segments

In 1998, Sharp focused on driving performance management throughout his organization. He established three main perspectives to "make stakeholders happy":

❶ The customer perspective

❷ The employee perspective

❸ The shareholder perspective

He then asked his teams to isolate monthly and quarterly goals and measures for each of these perspectives, which had to be balanced. He started with less complicated measures in each of the perspectives and focused them on continuous improvement as the company grew. He encouraged teams to develop and participate in establishing measures, assigning leaders, and developing a common dictionary of measures. He communicated these metrics, measures in companywide meetings but continued to be informal in his own formats to ease the transition into a new culture.

Sharp believes that strategy defines the direction an organization is going. Performance management defines the framework for execution and measurement of a deployed and mobilized strategy. Budgets merely reflect the capacity to execute the tactics. When Sharp, now Chairman of Triquint, was asked what he would do if he could do it all again, he said, "I would have done *that* earlier."

[a] Interview with Steve Sharp
[b] SWOT is a method and framework of strategic competitive analysis that outlines Strengths, Weaknesses, Opportunities, and Threats in the marketplace.

Assemble the Right Team Again

The team that brought BSC to the organization might not be the team that expands BSC to the enterprise. The initial team is usually populated with champions who are driven to transform the organization. They might drive for pilots to achieve results.

The team that pushes for enterprise BSC must have these characteristics:

- It is systematic about deployment of the knowledge and the system
- It is able to establish a long-term process of feedback and use of scorecards.

- It understands that the BSC system cannot cut corners and just prove a point.

- It is able to identify barriers and not just push them over for a short-term result. They must use continuous improvement methods to find solutions to challenging problems.

- It is able to adjust to the change in level of visibility. Instead of having a direct line to the management team, the new team must work without the power and attention of the chief executive.

Summary

Cascading the BSC project is not a simple issue but must be held to simplicity for it to work. Given that measures and objectives and initiatives and strategy linkage are all needed and coordinated, the challenge in a large enterprise is significant. Furthermore, enterprise deployment of BSC can take two forms:

1. A centrally controlled and modeled environment

2. A distributed environment

Both have their advantages and disadvantages, depending on the organizational demands. Central control places a significant burden on the team and does not provide for expanded learning with respect to building and maintaining a BSC system. However, it is certainly simpler to manage and implement. A distributed modeling environment allows for flexibility and for inputs to the models at local sites where the performance measures exist. This method might cause insistencies, and checking for consistencies and reporting under one umbrella could be challenging.

CHAPTER 12

Eleven Deadly Sins of Balanced Scorecard

After reading this chapter, you will be able to:

- Recognize the eleven deadly sins of scorecarding:
  - Five people-related sins
  - Three process-related sins
  - Three technology-related sins
- Have a strategy for overcoming the eleven deadly sins.

Organizations that succeed in their implementations anticipate and overcome the following eleven sins:

1. Taking the time to gather relevant data (a technology and process challenge)

2. Not making BSC a critical part of management process (a process challenge)

3. Stopping the education of users and managers (a people challenge)

4. Looking for the *Aha!* instead of the "I knew it!" (a process challenge)

5. Managing understanding and support (a people challenge)

6. Not fighting the freeloaders who resist change (a people challenge)

7. Searching for push-button solutions (a technological challenge)

8. Expecting the design to freeze (a technology challenge)

9. Assuming no hidden costs (a resource challenge)

10. Managing from the executive suite (a people management challenge)

11. Forgetting the values, vision, and mission (a process challenge)

Several of these challenges have been addressed in prior chapters, but it is important to stress the simplicity of solutions if anticipated and overcome even before they surface.

Taking the Time to Gather Relevant Data

Data gathering and data cleansing demands are challenging, but organizations are not suffering too little data. Someone, somewhere, somehow in the organization at any time is collecting point-oriented data. The challenge is to not reinvent the wheel. However, people are using performance measures everywhere that could be irrelevant to strategy. Stop them from this meaningless endeavor. Performance information that does not feed strategy is misdirected. Saddled with too much data, the skill is in identifying the correct and relevant sources of performance data and drivers.

Not Making the BSC a Critical Part of the Management Process

Organizations who have taken BSC to success have one thing in common—they made the methods a part of everyone's day-to-day functions. If not, the scorecard will turn into a political tool or one built to "game the system." Spyros Makridakis, author of *Forecasting, Planning and Strategy for the 21st Century*, declares that "in practice, the procedure, criteria, information, and measurement of results become a game of bending the rules and taking actions aimed only at improving the score."[1] These organizations drove the balanced scorecard from a methodology to a culture of communicating performance. In my organization, I drove the process of reporting on the scorecard weekly and ensured that a quarterly review of objectives at the beginning and the end of the process was followed consistently. This demanded considerable discipline but gave the team and the organization significance in reporting and management. Furthermore, it was the single most important method of management for the organization.

Stopping the Education of Users and Managers

Educating users is an unending challenge. Saturn President Richard G. "Skip" Lefaurve put it well when he declared, "If you think education is expensive, just try ignorance."[2] Prior chapters have discussed the value of educating users and have suggested alternatives as to how. Adding to this, the knowledge workers who understand the value and use of BSC will make decisions. The others will mistake BSC for another irrelevant tool. Conceptual and technical training are essential in the value and use of BSC but technical training is also important:

- *BSC fundamentals.* Learning the basics about BSC.
- *Case studies.* Learning from others' mistakes and successes is key to building a BSC program. Looking at cases in the industry being considered will bring a whole new light on the project. Not all industry implementations are similar and matching objectives to models is key.
- *Integrating data sources with an BSC System.* Almost 70 percent of the model is importable from various sources.
- *Optimizing and designing a BSC model.* Many times, models are built with very little forethought as to which is the best and most optimized way to work with the software.
- *Data mapping and cleansing.* Many projects underestimate the tedious work required when multiple datastreams are brought into one model. Unfortunately, the many organizational silos

store data in different syntax and formats. Data cleansing requires repetitive work and skill. Data mapping is the art of
linking all this data into one common model.

- *Collecting empirical information.* The trouble with collecting information is that it is not as exciting the second and third time.
Also, collecting information found in peoples' heads about
process and the work being done is even more challenging.
Technology can help in this process. Survey-based input software is available.

- *Sustaining models.* First time around, every BSC exercise seems
exciting and it would be easy to cut corners, skip a few formal-
ities, and get to the final result. However, the next time around,
and the next time after that, careful attention to detail and
knowledge to maintaining models is required.

- *Multimodel management.* Consider having ten models in ten
different countries whose results are reported on. Technology
exists and formalism exists to support this topology. But users
and maintainers of the system must keep up to date in their
learning and their motivation.

- *Consolidating models.* Many times many models in different
places need to be consolidated and combined to give a total
picture of the enterprise.

- *Designing a business intelligence or executive information system.* Flat
reports are fine, but technology now exists that can pour a model
into a cube so that users can "slice-and-dice" the information.
BSC data lends itself to this very well because all the information
contains hierarchy and cause and effect, and has depth.

- *Designing custom reports.* Reports still top the list of outputs for a
BSC model regardless of all the other ways to interrogate the
model.

- *Linking performance management to scorecards.* The world of performance measurement is open and wide with the introduction of Balanced Scorecard methodology.[3] Performance

management and scorecards/performance measurement systems feed each other. The technology now exists that links both of these functions together so that the cost and profitability elements of performance management can add to the vast performance measurement schemes established by organizations. Chapter 13 discusses this area.

Looking for the Aha! Instead of the "I Knew It!"

Much of the BSC process is not new realizations but reenforces the strategy into action across the entire organization. Unfortunately, new methods applied onto organizations tend to promise new insights. The *Aha!* syndrome, that is, the need to always reinforce the new and great insights, although in the process can destroy the operational consistency of an organization. The true value of BSC to a corporation is not new insights but the consistency of strategy reinforced into action.

Managing Understanding and Support

Management understanding and use can be achieved by reflecting the understanding of what is important for them. Strategy is in the hands of the management, while operational implementation is in the hands of the teams. Management's attention is highly elusive and must be focused for a BSC project to succeed. BSC projects must tie to strategy. The true custodians of strategy are the key managers and leaders in the organization and their attention to the BSC operational methods is essential for the continuity and institutionalization of the program. Some suggestions to include management in the process follow:

- Schedule regular meetings and discussions with management.

- Ensure that managers report using the scorecard as framework in all management meetings.

- Ensure that the highest level of managers and leaders publish their scorecards and objectives.

Not Fighting the Freeloaders Who Resist Change

People who enjoy the benefits of distorted information tend not to want change. Why should they confess to a change when they are finding themselves on the top of the value chain? In any organization, there are perceived winners and real winners. Real winners always look for real answers; perceived winners prefer status quo even when on the *Titanic*. Management endorsement and the apolitical encouragement will get past these barriers, but until then everyone wants problems to be some-one else's. The organization that resists any change should worry the champion. Without management support and a logical organizational culture, one should question the probability of success.

TIPS & TECHNIQUES

Fighting the Freeloaders

Freeloaders are ones who benefit from confusion and enjoy the lack of definition because they live in the blindness of the organization. The best ways to affect these freeloaders is to

- Expose them using the scorecard.

- Enable the winners by using the scorecard.

- Educate the nonsupporters as those that are adamantly unsupportive can be equally supportive when convinced.

- Use the management structure to ensure that these freeload-ers get on board or leave. They serve no purpose to the mis-sion, or the strategy except to hold back progress.

Searching for Push-Button Solutions

Push-button solutions have been the expectation of humans because they touched a computer. This will happen only if change never occurs. The nature of a BSC project is change—that is, when we use BSC we will change the structure of our work and the use of data will change periodically. Hence, push-button solutions tend not to be characteristic of a BSC system.

Expecting the Design to Freeze

Many an organization spends time to set up a BSC and finds that their pursuit of stability has led to even more instability because it has now found new ideas in new markets and must work even harder to catch up to the demands. Rather than a frozen model for success, it is left with a new, ever-changing model for growth. No one can anticipate the transformations that come about after results are shared. Hence, BSC practitioners may expect to redesign and rebuild their creations regularly. This would be a good problem to have. Organizations that consistently repopulate their models with the same data and report on them are suspicious. The real reason BSC exists is to change not just the data but also the structure of business and hence, the structure of the BSC model. Only then will related improvements surface. If no changes occur, the organization is static.

In a BSC exercise, tactics and go-to-market plans may shift as new market data and balanced information now exists to awaken the teams. Strategy must remain.

Assuming No Hidden Costs

Hidden costs can kill the continuity of your project. Consider the following costs in anticipating the resource requests of the project:

- Training and re-training costs
- Educational tools, for example, books and videos
- Consultant costs with possible overruns
- Software upgrades and updates
- User group attendance
- Visits to vendors
- Emergency calls and trips
- Integration technology costs
- Support schemes, for example, number of calls before the charges begin

Managing from the Executive Suite

Yvon Rousseau observed, in his article "Turning Strategy into Action in Financial Services,"[4] that the BSC can suffer from being the "executive toy" syndrome, identifying that BSC can be viewed as a top-down tool. If the process does not deliver both top-down and bottom-up communication, it can be seriously compromised. Measures must reach levels of the corporation that are really performing the work. I once worked for a very successful manager who said that all of the executives were overhead and the others did all the real work. These key individuals need to see cascaded objectives and measures that they can control and measure. If not, the "toy" will soon stop working.

Forgetting the Values, Vision, and Mission

Although the enthusiasm of BSC gathers steam and engulfs the organization in measurement and management methods, the ultimate aim of the process can get lost and the way in which the organization wishes to win may also lose direction. Organizations using BSC can forget the true purpose behind why they are doing BSC. Ultimately, it takes the CEO and the management team to remind all that the purpose is not to punish or to boast of a process. The purpose is to win the right way and to build resilience in the organization for change when needed. The framework is one that allows the organization a common understanding, a language and a formalism to communicate, correct, and to command the marketplace. Using the vision to see the future, the values to guide the actions and the mission to understand the targets, BSC is an instrument of strategy digestion not a means to measurement.

Summary

The eleven deadly sins of scorecarding identify a set of blind-spots that could affect the success of a BSC exercise:

- Taking the time to gather relevant data (a technology and process challenge)

- Not making BSC a critical part of management process (a process challenge)

- Stopping the education of users (a people challenge)

- Looking for the *Aha!* instead of the "I knew it!" (a process challenge)

- Managing understanding and support (a people challenge)

- Not fighting the freeloaders who resist change (a people challenge)

- Searching for push-button solutions (a technological challenge)

- Expecting the design to freeze (a technology challenge)

- Assuming no hidden costs (a resource challenge)

- Managing from the executive suite (a management challenge)

- Forgetting the values, vision, and mission (a process challenge)

CHAPTER 13

The Ultimate Partnership: Balanced Scorecard and Performance Management

After reading this chapter, you will be able to

- Understand what is performance management.

- Show how BSC assists in framing performance management.

- Recognize where BSC can assist organizations with uniquely new application demands.

In the last three decades, academics, consultants, and practitioners have ventured to identify, understand, and implement new and bold methods to do the following:

- *Optimize business processes* (e.g., business process re-engineering (BPR)).

- *Organize costs, quality, and time in business* (e.g., BPR, activity-based cost/management (ABC/M), and customer relationship management (CRM)).

- *Identify strategy management tools and philosophies* (e.g., BSC).

Performance Management and Measurement

Many of these developments have also spawned a business transformation and technological revolution of business intelligence, analytics, and enterprise resource planning (ERP) systems, along with billions of dollars of consulting. Underlying all this transformation is a category of business transformation called *performance management*. It has two particular areas of influence:

1. *Human performance management.* This category is about organizing work, people performance systems, and about benefits management.

TIPS & TECHNIQUES

Much of business intelligence and other analytics are sold as computer systems rather than process and methodology change and reinvention. Most organizations adopt performance management because they want to transform the way their corporation identifies, measures, and manages to goals. Many of the problems that have surfaced in business transition can be attributed to the lack of one clear understanding: Organizations must change processes and the way people work before computer systems can enable change.

"People before process" and "process before productivity" could be the mantra of the experienced change leader. Otherwise, you will speed up ineffective process. People drive every change in an organization, and the belief that one person cannot change a corporation is false. One single idea and one person with it can transform the entire personality of a corporation. Consider the following tips:

- Ensure that activities and processes are understood and changed.
- Ensure that teams understand the need for change and have adapted.
- Analyze the dimensions of cost, quality, and time prior to automating processes and functions.
- Work with people and get them to understand why you are pursuing the path you are. Try to understand their motivations in this transformation.

2. *Corporate performance management.* This category is about analytics, tools, systems, and methodologies around the financial, operational, and strategic performance of a corporation.

Performance management, in the BSC context, focuses primarily on the second area of influence. However, it has major implications to human performance management as well. Let's consider some examples of performance management methodology systems.

Business Process Re-engineering

Michael Hammer and Gary Hamel, the fathers of re-engineering, defined *business process re-engineering* to be the "fundamental rethinking and radical re-design of business processes to achieve dramatic improvements in critical, contemporary measures of performance, such as cost, quality, service, and speed.[1]

They outlined key words in this definition:

- Fundamental
- Radical
- Dramatic
- Processes

The world embraced this approach and took to it by storm. Today, many believe that more than 50 percent of these initiatives have not lived up to their claim. As early as 1994, U.S. companies spent approximately $32 billion on business re-engineering, and two-thirds failed. Yet, let's examine the re-engineering promise. Its promise was that dramatic results can be achieved by redesigning processes using contemporary performance measure. But many just redesigned processes to improve speed, instead of looking at what to improve first, using all contemporary measures available. A key contemporary measure of cost is ABC/M. With it, one can focus on areas of improvement rather than speed up efficiently that which is non–value-added in the first place. In many ways, ABC should be performed before any other initiative is engaged so that organizations can learn where to target their initiatives.

Activity-Based Cost/Management

Activity-based costing (ABC) was developed as a practical solution to managing overhead. In the 1980s, many companies, based on the finding[2] of Professor Robert Kaplan of Harvard Business School, Professors Robin Cooper and Tom Johnson of Portland State University, began to realize that traditional accounting systems and cost management methodologies were distorting how overhead should be associated with the product and services the company performed. This is not due to incorrectness but because the nature of overhead had transformed while the methods that treated overhead have not. Traditional systems did not evolve to support the changing behavior of costs. In the past, managers had to put up with this thing called *overhead* that they were charged to their departments, while they knew well that these costs were incorrectly allocated to them.

In the 1980s, the Consortium of Advanced Manufacturing-International (CAM-I) defined ABC as "a methodology that measures the costs and performance of activities, resources and cost objects."[3]

Spurred by lead articles and books from enlightened thought leaders[4] and a great need in the field for an answer to where overhead is going, ABC began to be viewed as an initiative in the 1990s. Unfortunately, it was billed as a replacement for then current cost management methods, and ABC began to take on the general ledger. This did not work. Even though the industry has moved beyond this, stigma still exists in the minds of new entrants and curious, new discoverers of ABC in the field. They ask, "Does it replace the GL?"

Beginning in the manufacturing industry, ABC served a strong need for firms that were struggling to identify a means of the following:

- Measuring how products and services consume overhead
- Understanding the true costs of activities within organizations
- Understanding the true costs of products and services
- Understanding the true profitability of channels, products, and services
- Quantifying, measuring, analyzing, and improving business processes

The early 1990s were filled with ABC endeavors that were billed as change initiatives that would re-engineer the finance output. These initiatives moved from the pure manufacturing companies to cover the process manufacturing industry, the service industry, and the government. They were generated out of visionary finance teams and champions targeted as a cost cutting initiative. Chief financial officers endorsed them as a way to improve the profitability death spirals of their corporations—or, in the case of government, to do more with less and to justify budgets. Likened to liposuction, ABC was used to identify dreaded overhead and assign this large and undefined beast into its correct cage. ABC served a strong purpose then because traditional cost methodologies tended to allocate costs directly to products and services with a single-stage allocation. Costs are allocated based on labor or standard

"Focusing" on Strategy and Cascading Objectives

InFocus Corporation, leader in digital projection, has been working with strategy alignment within its organization for the last decade or more. Driven by a one-page strategic map, InFocus has gone to the second phase of deploying objectives, key performance indicators, and scorecards to all levels of the worldwide organization.

As usual in many corporations, the challenge in building cohesion depends on the many cultures and silos within the corporation. Under the leadership of veteran John Harker, key management teams are instituting key strategic themes grounded in a modified form of Balanced Scorecard. Armed with three strategic themes, balanced with several perspectives unique to InFocus, the leadership is encouraging its operations to focus on translating strategy to action worldwide.

There are several key lessons on making strategy everyone's work:

- It is just as important to reinforce learning and coaching within the corporation as it is to formulate strategy and objectives.

- Strategy and objectives can be deployed worldwide at the same time. Key managers travel personally to worldwide locations to deliver key strategic messages and procedures to ensure that no miscommunication occurs and to model the importance of alignment.

- Human resources play a key role in the learning, negotiating of objectives, and measures between manager and teams.

- Communication is key in all that they do. Special sessions are held regularly to discuss strategy and objectives, and managers at all levels are expected to champion management, measurement, and direction setting.

overhead volume drivers. Labor hours, traditionally, being the larger portion of total overhead mix, would drive the decision of where to put overhead costs.

An historic description of the evolution of ABC is found in *Implementing Activity-Based Management in Daily Operations* by John Miller[5], and in *Ernst & Young Guide to Total Cost Management* by M.R. Ostrenga, Terrence R. Osan, Robert D. Mcilhartan, and Marcus D. Harwood.[6] *Activity-Based Information Systems: An Executive's Guide to Implementation* is another useful resource.[7]

Business Intelligence and Analytics

There is no end to the number of systems vendors and consulting firms who are focused onto business intelligence and analytics. Some are oriented toward visualization tools, while others are focused on the underlying infrastructure and data environment. These tools are rooted in the dream of making data into decisions. They are at the heart of the information revolution. Supply chain management (SCM) has moved to the forefront of business analytics and has captured the imagination of many organizations whose life-blood flows in their logistics to and from the customer. SCM is the science and art of driving value through the value-chain, be it ensuring that shoes get to market or groceries get through the broker, retailer, or manufacturer chain rapidly and with the least overhead costs.

How BSC Fits in the Continuum of Performance Management Infrastructure

Much of business transformation methods are disjoint and lack clarity in cohesion. BSC can be the umbrella that integrates the business units of an organization. As many of these business transformation initiatives are found in operations or finance, BSC can bring these to light and give them purposeful connections to the strategic management of the corporation. Many operational and financial initiatives suffer from two main challenges:

1. The lack of alignment with the CEO attention

2. The lack of alignment with strategy of the organization

The amazing value of BSC is that it connects the boardroom to the boiler room. It ensures that the analytics performed at lower levels with the organization feeds the overall strategic map of the entire organization. It can, in certain instances, create and drive the need for other performance management initiatives across the organization, that is, the scorecard may demand information not yet available in the organization and an ABC/M program may need to be launched to find the information.

However, the value of doing BSC first is that the organization can design the other performance management expectations based on strategic themes rather than just driving tactical efficiencies. Both are important.

Unique Applications of BSC

Competitive Intelligence (CI) and BSC

Many companies tend to view BSC as a framework for viewing and designing their own strategic direction. In my practice, I ask organizations to identify, draw, and gain insight into their competitors using the BSC framework. Using the four perspectives, teams can consider their competitions' strategic themes and consider what and how they measure. This exercise does illustrate how little organizations know about the strategy of their competitors. BSC helps CI teams, throughout Fortune 1000 companies, focus on the key strategic competitive differentiators rather than just gathering tactical information constantly. Furthermore, BSC is usually done with no concept of the competition until the customer perspective is discussed. Starting with competitive BSC will get the corporation to understand the uniqueness of the strategy upon which it is embarking.

In other words, organizations can differentiate themselves not just in their strategic view of the market but also in the unique way the company organizes its perspectives into key steps and measures.

Getting on "Board" with BSC

Corporate governance is a key issue for public companies. Most tools and methodologies for governance are driven by finances, as in the auditing committees, and people, as in the compensation committees.

What about strategy governance? "One of the major outputs of good governance is establishing boards that understand the strategy of the organization and the risks associated with that strategy . . ."[8] says R. W. Dye, CEO of CMA Canada. He continues, "Adopting a Balanced Scorecard for a board of directors would help address this situation."

How much of the information given to boards is "historical financial reports rather than future-oriented information?"[9] In some ways, boards have been managing by using lagging indicators rather than leading. BSC can enable boards to follow strategic themes, maps, and actions. They can hold the CEO accountable for transferring strategy to the teams, and they can use BSC's common language to communicate among each other and to the teams.

Summary

BSC can be used for several key strategic activities besides aligning strategy to action or measuring the performance of the organization.

- *Understand what is performance management.* Performance management, in the context of financial and strategic performance, is the science and art of business performance improvement. Performance management is a set of methodologies applied within organizations to dramatically improve their performance. Budgeting, planning, activity-based cost/management, balanced scorecard are examples of such methods. The real value from these disciplines comes when they work in concert toward a strategic imperative, for example, drive costs out of customer service.

- *Show how BSC assists in framing performance management.* BSC is the basis for bringing a strategic focus to any performance management project. Several ABC/M programs have failed to be sustainable because they did not link to strategic imperatives. BSC is a framework for driving all other performance management projects because its premise is to bring strategy into focus at the operational level.

- *Recognize where BSC can assist organizations with uniquely new application demands.* BSC can be used for several other programs within the corporation. A few examples discussed were:

  - A framework for competitive intelligence.
  - A framework for board governance.

Balanced Scorecard, like other frameworks and management tools, is not a replacement for good management. It is a consistent model for strategic focus within the corporation or group. Balanced Scorecard, if implemented consistently throughout the corporation, forms the basis upon which a great strategy, a motivating mission, and a good management team can grow the corporation.

Endnotes

Chapter 1

1. Dava Sobel, *Longitude* (New York: Penguin Books, 1995).

2. Robert S. Kaplan and David P. Norton, *The Balanced Scorecard* (Boston: Harvard Business School Press, 1996).

3. Michael Porter, "What Is Strategy," *Harvard Business Review* (November–December 1996).

4. W. Chan Kim and Renee Mauborgne, "Value Innovation: The Strategic Logic of High Growth," *Harvard Business Review* (January–February 1997), p. 106.

5. Michael Tracy and Fred Wiersema, *The Discipline of Market Leaders* (Boston: Addison-Wesley Publishing, 1995).

6. D. Garvin, "Interview with Craig Weatherup of Pepsi: Leveraging Processes for Strategic Advantage," *Harvard Business Review* (September–October 1995).

Chapter 2

1. John Purcell, Nick Kinnie, and Sue Hutchinson, *People Management* (May 2003), pp. 31–33.

2. Peter Drucker, *Managing in a Time of Great Change* (New York: TT Dutton, 1993), p. 118.

3. Douglas Smith, *Make Success Measurable* (New York: John Wiley & Sons, Inc., 1999), p. 14.

4. Robert Kaplan and David P. Norton, *Balanced Scorecard* (Boston: Harvard Business School Press, 1996).

5. Howard Armitage and Cam Scholey, "Mapping Mavens: How Private and Public Companies Gain from Strategic Mapping," *CMA* (May 2003), pp. 15–18.

6. Deborah L. Kerr, "The Balanced Scorecard in the Public Sector," *Perform Magazine* 1, no. 8, pp. 4–9.

Chapter 3

1. Christopher Meyer, "How the Right Measures Help Teams Excel," *Harvard Business Review* (May–June 1994), p. 95.

2. Rich Willis, "Major Boo-Boo," *Forbes ASAP* (April 7, 1997), p. 36.

3. Gary H. Anthes, "The Long Arm of Moore's Law," *Computerworld* (October 5, 1998), p. 69. *Note about Moore's Law:* Mr. Gordon Moore is founder of Intel Corporation. He identified this theory, which is used extensively to identify the growth of semiconductor complexity.

4. Fay A. Borthick and Harold Roth, "Faster Access to More Information for Better Decisions," *Journal of Cost Management* (Winter 1997), p. 25.

5. Peter Drucker presented this notion in his keynote speech at the Annual Users Group meeting for Cognos Corporation in 1997.

6. Lawrence S. Lyons, "Creating Tomorrow's Organization: Unlocking the Benefits of Future Work," *Leader to Leader* (Summer 1997), pp. 7–9. "A gap existed between the needs of the business and the capabilities of technology. Today all that has changed. The capabilities of information technology now outstrip the needs of business."

7. Peter Drucker, "The Information Executives Truly Need," *Harvard Business Review* (January–February 1995), pp. 54–62.

8. John Whitney, "Strategic Renewal for Business Units," *Harvard Business Review* (July–August 1996), p. 85.

9. Morris Treadway, *A Primer on Activity-Based Management: ABM in Utilities; A Process for Managing a Market Driver Business* (Coopers & Lybrand, 1995).

10. John H. Lingle and William A. Schiermann, "From Balanced Scorecard to Strategic Gauges: Is Measurement Worth It?" *Management Review* 85, no. 3 (March 1996), p. 56.

11. Christopher D. Ittner and David F. Larcker, "Coming Up Short on Nonfinancial Performance Measures," *Harvard Business Review* (November 2003).

Chapter 4

1. Webster's 9th New Collegiate Dictionary (Springfield, MA: Merriam Webster Inc., 1991).

2. Michael Porter,"What Is Strategy?" *Harvard Business Review* (November–December 1996), pp. 61–78.

3. C. K. Prahalad and Gary Hamel, "The Core Competence of the Corporation," *Harvard Business Review* (May–June 1990).

4. Ibid.

5. C. K. Prahalad and Gary Hamel, *Competing for the Future* (Boston: Harvard Business School Press, 1994).

6. Interview and follow-up e-mail from Deborah Kerr, Texas state auditor's office.

7. Mission Statement from Qsent. Used with permission.

8. Deborah Kerr, "The Balanced Scorecard in the Public Sector," *Perform Magazine* 1, no. 8, pp. 4–9.

9. James R. Lucas, *Fatal Illusions* (AMACOM, 1997), p. 40.

Chapter 5

1. John H. Lingle and William A. Schiemann, "From Balanced Scorecard to Strategic Gauges; Is Measurement Worth It?" *Management Review* 85, no. 3 (March 1996), p. 55.

Chapter 6

1. Charles Fishman, "Change," *Fast Company* (April–May 1997), p. 66.

2. Andrew Grove, *High Output Management* (New York: Random House, 1983), p. 173.

3. Jim Collins, *Good to Great* (New York: HarperCollins, 2001) p. 57.

4. Peter M. Senge, *The Fifth Discipline* (New York: Doubleday Currency, 1990).

5. Steven Covey, *The 7 habits of Highly Effective People* (New York: Simon & Schuster Inc., 1990).

6. Thomas D. Davenport, "Information Behavior: Why We Build Systems That Users Won't Use," *Computerworld* (September 15, 1997), p. 3.

Chapter 7

1. J. Whitney, "Strategic Renewal for Business Units," *Harvard Business Review* (July–August 1996), pp. 84–98.

2. Georgia M. Harrigan and Ruth E. Miller, "Managing Change through an Aligned and Cascading Balanced Scorecard: A Case Study" (courtesy of Pbviews at *www.pbview.com*).

3. Bala Balachandran, "Cost Management at Saturn: A Case Study," *Business Week Executive Briefing Services* 5, pp. 25–28.

4. James C. Collins and Jerry I. Porras, *Built To Last: Successful Habits of Visionary Companies* (New York: HarperCollins, 1994).

Chapter 8

1. Balanced Scorecard Collaborative, *www.bscol.com*.

2. Christopher Dedera, "Harris Semiconductor ABC: Worldwide Implementation and Total," *Journal of Cost Management* (Spring 1996), p. 94.

3. Adapted from K. Phillips and Kevin Dilton-Hill, "Willards Foods: Managing Customer Profitability with ABC Information," *As Easy as ABC: ABC Technologies Newsletter* (Winter 1996).

4. Steven Covey, *The 7 Habits of Highly Effective People* (New York: Simon & Schuster, 1990).

5. Thomas Hoffman, "Datawarehouse, the Sequel," *Computerworld* (June 2, 1997), pp. 69–72.

6. Report mining systems generate asynchronous reports that are self-triggering when certain predefined data items or formulae or relationships change. Read Stewart Mckie, "Mining Your Accounting Data," *Controller Magazine* (November 1996), pp. 43–46.

Chapter 9

1. Brenk Lank, "Performance Measurement System for Subaru-Isuzu Automotive Inc.," Pbview case study, *www.pbviews.com*.

2. Shaku Atre, "Plan for Data Marts," *Computerworld* (June 16, 1997), pp. 71–72.

Chapter 10

1. Brent Lank, "Performance Measurement System for Subaru-Isuzu Automotive Inc.," case study on *www.pbviews.com*.

2. XML = eXtendable markup language used for the interchange of structured data. Designed for interoperatability and ease of design.

3. Major Peter Bishop, Major Karl Leclerc, "Implementing Performance Measurement within a Government Organization," case study on *www.pbviews.com*.

4. EVA is a registered trademark of Stern Stewart & Co.

5. CJ McNair, "To Serve The Customer Within," *Journal of Cost Management* (Winter 1996), p. 42.

Chapter 11

1. Paul R. Niven, *Balanced Scorecard, Step-by-Step: Maximizing Performance and Maintaining Results* (New York: John Wiley & Sons, Inc., 2002).

2. Exhibits 11.3, 11.4, and 11.5 are only prototypes of a possible BSC reporting system and are not meant to be endorsed in any way. They are merely used as samples for reader. Microsoft Access is a trademark of Microsoft Corp.

Chapter 12

1. Spyros G. Makridakis, *Forecasting, Planning, and Strategy for the 21st Century* (New York: Free Press, 1990), p. 233.

2. Bala Balachandran, "Cost Management at Saturn: A Case Study," *Business Week Executive Briefing Services* 5, pp. 25–28.

3. Robert S. Kaplan and David P. Norton, *The Balanced Scorecard* (Boston: Harvard Business School Press, 1996).

4. Yvon Rousseau, "Turning Strategy into Action in Financial Services," *SMA Management* 73, no. 10 (December 1999/January 2000), p. 25.

Chapter 13

1. M. Hammer, M and J. Champy, *Reengineering the Corporation* (New York: HarperBusiness, 1993).

2. Some treatment of the topic can also be found in J. Miller and T. Vollman, "The Hidden Factory," *Harvard Business Review* (September–October 1985).

3. Norm Raffish, and Peter B.B. Turney, ed., *The CAM-I Glossary of Activity-Based Management, version 1.2* (Arlington, TX: The Consortium for Advanced Manufacturing—International, 1992).

4. H. Thomas Johnson and Robert S. Kaplan, *Relevance Lost: The Rise and Fall of Management Accounting* (Boston: Harvard Business School Press, 1987).

5. J. Miller, *Implementing Activity-Based Management in Daily Operations* (New York: John Wiley & Sons, Inc., 1996).

6. M.R. Ostrenga, Terrence R. Osan, Robert D. Mcilhartan, Marcus D. Harwood, *Ernst & Young Guide to Total Cost Management* (New York: John Wiley & Sons, Inc., 1992).

7. Mohan Nair, *Activity-based Information Systems: An Executive's Guide to Implementation* (New York: John Wiley & Sons, Inc., 1999).

8. R.W. Dye, "Keeping Score," *CMA Management* (December/January 2003), pp. 18–23.

9. Dana R. Hermanson, and Heather M. Hermanson, "The Balance Scorecard as a Board Tool," *Corporate Board* 10, no. 102 (January/February 1997), p. 17.

Glossary

Activity-based cost/management (ABC/M)   An alterative to traditional accounting methods, providing an activity view of where overhead is assigned in businesses, reducing the general distortion often suffered. This model, introduced by Professors Bob Kaplan and Tom Johnson, has grown to be an understood method for costing products and services in the Global 100.

Balanced Scorecard (BSC)   A formalism, methodology, and framework that translates strategy to actionable and measurable objectives. Following four perspectives, BSC balances these objectives among nonfinancial and financial, leading and lagging, operations and finance, as example. This methodology allows for all parts of the organization to know and understand their contribution to strategy.

Benchmarking   Comparing metrics between companies or peer organizations.

Cascading the scorecard   The action of driving objectives, measures, targets, and initiatives into the organization and through multiple levels.

Cause and effect   The effect of recognizing the relationship among strategic themes and their impact on one another.

Champion   A person who is tasked or has taken the role of motivating, articulating change and organizing business transformation.

Core competency   The basic set of capabilities and habits a corporation has that is unique to its personality and skills.

Data obesity   A phenomenon in which organizations are inundated with data at all levels and cannot use it or understand its value.

Information starved   A phenomenon in which organizations are unable to discover relevance in the information they have to work with.

Initiatives   The key programs an organization must undertake to enable objectives to be achieved. Some take the form of change programs like ISO 9000 or leadership training.

Key performance indicators   Known in the industry as essential measures that are critical for strategic or tactical realization.

Lagging indicator   A measure(s) that is identified only after an event occurs.

Leading indicator   A measure(s) that can indicate the result of an event prior to it occurring.

Learning adoption cycle   The process of moving an organization through four phases:

1. *Trigger phase.* An event that forces everyone to take a second look at solving problems.
2. *Education phase.* The process of learning of solutions to the existing problems to answer the question, "What is it?"
3. *Pilot phase.* The process of testing the solution in a small unit or section of the organization to answer the question, "Does it work for me?"
4. *Production phase.* The process of moving into a sustainable enterprise model with the question, "Can it work continuously?"

Measure   A quantifiable formula whose variables define what needs to be measured and monitored in order that a target is achieved.

Mission   Why an organization exists and what it is charged with.

Objective   A goal to be achieved that is specific, measurable, actionable, results in an achievement ends in a period of time.

OLAP   An on-line analytic processing. Database methodology that is a way to view multidimensional information. Software exists to ease this process.

Operational excellence   Doing an activity well.

Organizational resilience   The innate ability of an organization to take change and make change without destroying the key strategic themes it is targeted toward. The strength in an organization that can change its strategic themes and see it reflected in actions and corresponding performance measures.

Performance measure   The methods to align performance results to measures and to manage this process.

Performance measure dictionary   A document that collects, describes, and manages all the descriptions and connections in a set of measures of performance of a corporation.

Perspectives   BSC describes four main perspectives to consider in formulating strategic directions:

1. *Financial perspective.* Key financial objectives that define the overall strategic themes achievement.
2. *Customer perspective.* Issues of value, competency, and customer-related objectives.
3. *Internal perspective.* Operational, channel, and group objectives that lead and support the financial and customer goals.
4. *Learning and growth perspective.* The objectives that feed all other perspectives as the foundation for mobilizing and sustaining the organization is strategy realization.

Strengths, weaknesses, opportunities, and threats (SWOT) analysis   A method and framework of strategic competitive analysis that outlines strengths, weaknesses, opportunities, and threats in the marketplace.

Strategic paradox   The syndrome in which the management team of an organization believes that strategy is being executed in one fashion while the real activities of an organization are performed counter or different to the strategy.

Strategic positioning   Performing similar activities differently while capturing customer attention and value.

Strategic theme   Key strategic objectives for differentiation, focus, and market dominance.

Strategic thrust   See strategic theme.

Strategic variable   Key drivers and assumptions to strategy themes that, once changed or altered, can affect the validity of the strategy.

Strategy mapping   The process of linking all the strategic objectives within the four perspectives into a cause-and-effect map.

Target   A numeric or nonnumeric value representing a desired result.

Task-relevant leadership   The leadership qualities that fit the necessary skills required to complete a task.

Task-relevant readiness   The combination of characteristics that, if taken together, forms the basis of being ready for transformation. The elements that make this readiness are:

- Collect the ingredients to project ignition.

- Align the program to the organizational personality.

- Educate the enterprise.

- Move from agreement to commitment.

Value proposition   Usually associated with products and services, this is the emotional, symbolic, and practical residue after a customer envisions payment for a product or service.

Values   In contrast to a mission, which is *why* an organization exists, the values are about *how* an organization wishes to exist.

Vision   The sight of the mind. An organizational vision is the statement of what an organization sees as the state of the future.

Suggested Readings

Balanced Scorecard

Becker, B.E., M.A. Huselid, and D. Ulrich. *The HR Scorecard*. Boston: Harvard Business School Press, 2001.

Kaplan, Robert S., and David Norton. *The Balanced Scorecard*. Boston: Harvard Business School Press, 1996.

——. *The Strategy-Focused Organization*. Boston: Harvard Business School Press, 2001.

Niven, Paul R. *Balanced Scorecard, Step-by-Step for Government and Nonprofit Agencies*. Hoboken, NJ: John Wiley & Sons, Inc., 2003.

——. *Balanced Scorecard, Step-by-Step: Maximixing Performance and Maintaining Results*. New York: John Wiley & Sons, Inc., 2002.

Activity-Based Cost/Management

Johnson, Thomas H., and Bob Kaplan. *Relevance Lost: The Rise and Fall of Management Accounting*. Boston: Harvard Business School Press, 1987.

Kaplan, Robert S., and Robin Cooper. *Cost and Effect*. Boston: Harvard Business School Press, 1998.

Nair, Mohan. *Activity-based Information Systems: An Executive's Guide to Implementation*. New York: John Wiley & Sons, Inc., 1999.

Other Suggested Readings

Balachandran, Bala. "Cost Management at Saturn: A Case Study." *BusinessWeek Executive Briefing Services* 5 (1994), pp. 25–28.

Fishman, Charles. "Change." *Fast Company* (April 1995).

Hamel, Gary and C. K. Prahalad. *Competing for the Future*. Boston: Harvard Business School Press, 1994.

———. "Strategic Intent." *Harvard Business Review* (May–June 1989).

Kim, W. Chan, and Renee Mauborgne. "Value Innovation: The Strategic Logic of High Growth." *Harvard Business Review* (January–February 1997).

Ohmae, Kenichi. "Getting Back to Strategy." *Harvard Business Review* (November–December 1988).

Porter, Michael E. *Competitive Advantage: Creating and Sustaining Superior Performance*. New York: Free Press, 1985.

———. *Competitive Strategy: Techniques for Analyzing Industries and Competitors*. New York: Free Press, 1980.

———. "What Is Strategy?" *Harvard Business Review* (November–December 1996), pp. 61–78.

Schiemann, William, and John Lingle. "Seven Greatest Myths of Measurement." *Management Review* (May 1997), p. 29.

Informational Websites and Sample Vendor List

www.2emerge.com	Author's Web site
www.Bettermanagement.com	Performance management portal
www.bscol.com	Balance Scorecard Collaborative
www.cognos.com	Cognos Inc.—Corporate performance management vendor
www.comshare.com	Gaec (formerly called Comshare)
www.corvu.com	Corvu Corporation—Enterprise performance management
www.crystaldecisions.com	Crystal Decisions—Business intelligence vendor
www.gentia.com	Gentia—also BalancedScorecard.com
www.hbsp.harvard.edu	Harvard Business online
www.hyperion.com	Hyperion—Business performance management software vendor
www.oracle.com	Oracle—Enterprise resource planning vendor
www.pbviews.com	Panorama Business Views—Performance management vendor
www.peoplesoft.com	PeopleSoft—Enterprise resource planning vendor
www.prodacapo.com	ProDacapo
www.qpronline.com	QPR software LLC.

www.sap.com	SAP—Enterprise resource planning vendor
www.sas.com	SAS Corporation—Enterprise analytic vendor
www.wiley.com	John Wiley—Book publisher
www.cam-i.org	Consortium of Advanced Manufacturing International

Index